THE ABODE OF LOVE

D0723673

Kate Barlow was born in Egypt, where her father was serving with the British forces, and grew up in England. Between 1960 and 1965, she served in the Women's Royal Air Force and later became a newspaper reporter. In 1980, she moved to Canada, where she still resides with her family.

The Abode of Love

The remarkable tale of growing up in a religious cult

KATE BARLOW

MAINSTREAM PUBLISHING

EDINBURGH AND LONDON

This paperback edition published 2007

Copyright © Kate Barlow, 2006
All rights reserved
The moral right of the author has been asserted

First published in Great Britain in 2006 by
MAINSTREAM PUBLISHING COMPANY (EDINBURGH) LTD
7 Albany Street
Edinburgh EH1 3UG

ISBN 9781845962135

No part of this book may be reproduced or transmitted in any
form or by any other means without permission in writing from
the publisher, except by a reviewer who wishes to quote brief
passages in connection with a review written for insertion in a
magazine, newspaper or broadcast

A catalogue record for this book is available from the British Library

Typeset in Caslon

Printed in Great Britain by
Cox & Wyman Ltd, Reading

To

my sons,

Richard and Andrew

Acknowledgements

I was a new and very homesick immigrant to Canada in 1980 when I met Liz Jackson, who had arrived from England five years before me. Our friendship grew and I began telling her about my strange childhood, a subject I had pushed to the back of my mind for 20 years. 'You ought to write a book,' she said one day.

And so I have – eventually. Here it is, Liz, and thank you for your continuing friendship – and all the adventures we have already shared!

Liz was the first of a parade of people who have helped me reach this amazing point of publication. Neighbour Ann Pallant typed my first manuscript and later transcribed several tape recordings of survivors of the Abode of Love. Former Covent Garden opera diva Jean Watson, the late Jean Vernon, taught me never to give up – and never to split an infinitive, among my many egregious writing errors she spotted. I thank Estelle Salata, creative writing instructor at Sheridan College, Oakville, and members of our short-lived writing club, who listened kindly to my early attempts; the editors and fellow reporters at the *Hamilton Spectator*, who taught me more about how to tell a story than I shall probably ever realise; former managing editor John Gibson, who gave me my chance in daily newspapers; and, more recently, Casey Kostanje, former pastor and writer on religion, who waded through my grandfather's printed sermons in an effort to make sense of them for me.

That brings me to Canada, this vast, beautiful land, filled with people with generous hearts. My adopted country allowed me to put distance between myself and my childhood home, giving me the perspective I needed to write my story, and at the same time the opportunity to pursue my dream of becoming a newspaper reporter, ironically the one profession despised by my family – with good reason, I have to admit.

I thank the late Captain and Misses Burridge, who ran the long-gone St Hilda's School in Otterhampton, Somerset, where I boarded for 13 years – the only school I ever attended – for their unstinting selflessness in welcoming odd little pupils like me, as well as nurturing our spirits and instilling in us respect for the English language.

Without the help of those former school friends who visited my strange childhood home during the holidays, among them Pam Cooper (née Sheldrake), Diana Hawkins and Lesley Swinburn (née Chapman), I would surely not have been able to recall all those adventures we shared – and all the mischief we got up to. Thank you all so much, and also Hans and Trudel Lederman, the first outsiders to live within the walls of the Abode of Love, who recalled much that I had almost forgotten.

Thanks must also go to Spaxton historian the late Bert Harris, who not only built my grandfather's astonishingly ornate coffin but also had the good sense to collect memorabilia and memories of my childhood home; to genealogical researcher Andrew Froom of Bristol, who dug deep into my family tree to help sort truth from myth; to my nephew Jonathan Buckley for his help with the photographs and also his wife, Sally, who combed through a year's worth of newspapers to find the source of a single quote I needed;

and to Reverend Pam Schroder of the Ancient Catholic Church for her notes on the architectural features of the Ark of the Covenant.

I thank the authors of past volumes on the Abode of Love, who filled in many gaps in my knowledge and understanding. A heartfelt thanks also goes to Dr Joshua Schwieso, whose Ph.D. thesis on my childhood home provided a wealth of stunningly accurate background information and contributed wonderfully to my knowledge of those I grew up among.

How glad I am I enlisted Trisha Benesh of Author-Assist of California to help me get my manuscript into saleable shape. And what fun it has been to work under the guidance of the unfailingly helpful staff at Mainstream Publishing of Edinburgh, especially editor Deborah Warner, whose questions always made sense and whose suggestions for improvement have done just that. Thanks to Roger Richards for his help with the picture section and to Tim Goffe for the photographs of the stained-glass windows at the Ark of the Covenant.

Thanks go to the North Somerset Museum, Somerset County Council, UCL Hospitals NHS Trust, the British Library and the University of Nottingham for their assistance also.

And now to my family. My sisters, Ann and Margaret, are owed special mention, not just for the shared experiences binding us together to this day but for the love they have always shown their 'little sister'. I thank Ann for her determination in not letting us drift apart even though separated by an ocean. I also owe her special thanks for her foresight in removing from our childhood home that great trunk of photos and papers that we look through periodically, and especially the Agapemone (pronounced Ag-a-pem-on-e) diary, which forms a framework for my recollections. To Margaret, though we see each other less often, thank you for your ability to recapture that camaraderie from our childhood whenever we are together – and dust off those cherished memories. I've tried my best to recall events accurately and can only plead the intervening 50 years as a defence against any errors.

I thank my two sons, Richard and Andy, for their unwavering belief that I would finally succeed in my ambition to write a book.

And above all, I thank Ivor, my husband of 40 years, for his love and support, not to mention his cheerful acceptance of my strange past.

Perhaps I should end with a thank you to all those extraordinary people who lived, loved and died in the 'A', especially – albeit ambivalently – my dangerously charismatic grandfather, without whom there would be no book. I shall never forget the elderly and eccentric women I lived among and who taught me so much about acceptance and loyalty. My childhood may have been 'peculiar' but it was surrounded and buoyed up by love. What more can a child ask?

The true heroine of this book is surely my mother Lavita, who, in her own dogged way, succeeded in achieving for her daughters freedom from a past from which she never managed to escape.

In the nine months since publication of *The Abode of Love*, I have been touched by the many letters and emails I have received from readers. In one case, it was to ask for reassurance that a relative who long ago had abandoned her family to follow my grandfather had indeed been content with her decision. Another sent photos I had never seen before of my childhood home. But it was the emails from relatives I never knew existed that have astounded and delighted me. I am now in touch with Nick Harper, my grandmother Ruth's great nephew and my second cousin. I have met with Penny Smyth-Pigott and her sister Ann. They are my third cousins, once removed, on my grandfather Beloved's side of the family! From the moment we met, we all felt we had known each other all our lives. What a wonderful journey this has been.

And so, here it is. My story.

Contents

'. . . word, of course, spread round like lightning. I mean to say, you're asking for trouble if you go around saying things like that. Well, of course, there were hundreds of people waiting for us. They were shouting and roaring. I whipped the coach round smartly and headed for home . . . The mob chased us right across Clapton Common shouting "hypocrite" and things like that – a lot worse than that. When we got to Smyth-Pigott's house, he and his missus nipped in smartly . . .'

My grandfather's former coachman, Alfred Rawlings, aged 82, recalling the riots of half a century earlier, published in the *Daily Express*, 16 December 1955

1

The Cracked Dish

Soft rain. Water tanks on roof cleaned.

Entry in the Agapemone diary on
Tuesday, 24 February 1948

Twelve pairs of eyes!

Eleven old ladies and my sister. And they were all staring at me. I didn't know how Margaret had made it to the dining room so fast. We had been playing on the swing on the upper lawn when the quarter-to-one bell had rung. Even though she was five years older than me, and a much faster runner, she mustn't have washed her hands or brushed her hair to have got there so quickly. I knew Ann wouldn't be there. At nearly 14 she was deemed 'sensible' enough to lunch with our mother and grandmother.

'You're late, Catherine.' Eighty-six-year-old Emily Hine glared from her seat near the head of the long dining table. The elastic edge of the hair net she wore over her yellowy-white hair gave her an extra frown. Her jet necklaces jangled on her ample chest as she took a noisy disapproving breath and boomed, 'Again!'

I hated her calling me Catherine, even though it was my real name

– Catherine Jane Read, to be exact; I preferred Kitty. But I was far too scared to argue with this impressive old lady, who favoured fox furs with grinning heads and boot-button eyes on the rare occasions she ventured beyond the community walls.

'Sorry, Emily.' I stared at my scuffed shoes and fallen knee socks. I stole a glance at Margaret, sitting smugly in her seat near our nanny, Waa. My sister's big brown eyes – far larger than Ann's or mine – were alight with mischief. If she pulled one of her faces, I would giggle.

A watery sun shone through the tall windows, filling with a soft light what was the biggest dining room in the world. The light bounced off the huge gilt-framed mirrors hanging above the marble fireplaces at each end of the room and made the heavy silver cutlery and huge cruets on the long table glow rather than sparkle. The table seated 30 and still left room for an upright piano and a 'withdrawing area' of sofas and wing chairs.

I hurried to my seat between Waa and another of my favourite old ladies, 92-year-old Alice Bacon, who made sailboats out of squares of coloured paper, which I was allowed to launch in the birdbath in my grandmother's private garden.

Everyone was watching me. And not just those seated at the table. 'Dear Belovèd', as everyone called our grandfather, followed my every move with his sad, soulful eyes. Wearing a dark suit with a stiff collar and with his grey hair parted in the middle, he stared down at his dwindling flock from his portrait above the ornate mahogany sideboard. He had 'passed over', as everyone there called dying, when my mother was just 17, but his picture was everywhere: above the huge dining-room sideboard, high on the parlour wall, above the stairs leading to 'Granny's End'. Everyone kept telling my sisters and me how wonderful he was. I thought he looked sad and . . . was it lonely? But that didn't make sense, I told myself, as I slid into my seat. He had been surrounded by lots of people, all of whom loved him very much, so he could never have been lonely. I would be grown-up before

I would begin to understand the sentiment that lay behind my grandfather's enigmatic expression in the portrait.

'She wasn't very late this time,' bellowed enormous Olive Morris. Her ear trumpet, which she had painted to look like an African snake, swung as she turned to get her sister's attention.

'You're shouting,' mouthed her sister. As petite as Olive was large, Violet had been one of England's first women architects, something her sister informed me of regularly with pride.

'She's always shouting,' I heard someone mutter.

I stared at one of the mantelpieces and its display of bronze hunting dogs with dead rabbits dangling from their jaws. Normally I never looked at them, especially if rabbit was on the menu. But I had grown bored of counting chairs – 12 being sat on and 18 not being sat on.

I bowed my head and shut my eyes in preparation for grace. I didn't want to attract any more attention. One day when I hadn't shut my eyes, Emily had noticed and told me off. She must have been peeping too, to catch me.

'For what we are about to receive may we be truly thankful,' intoned Violet.

As if on cue, the dining-room door opened and in came Ethel, the housekeeper, followed in procession by Lettit and Cissy, two tiny Welsh sisters. The three elderly women, worn pinafores covering their old-fashioned dresses, each carried a large porcelain dish. These dishes were covered by Victorian silver domes to prevent the food getting too cold on its long journey from the kitchens. I guessed it would be cold mutton for lunch. It had been hot mutton yesterday. I didn't like either. I had thought about smuggling our Great Dane, Gay, into the dining room and slipping her my meat, but she was too big to go under the table. So now I was faced with a mealtime pushing slices of gristly mutton around my plate and trying to make them disappear.

Ethel knew I disliked meat, so she served me the smallest slice she could find on the huge porcelain platter, and Lettit and Cissy both let me take more than my fair share of boiled cabbage and potatoes. I spooned on a lake of mint sauce to disguise the meat, but it merely turned the fat a bilious green.

Absorbed in the movements of these pale green globs, I jumped at Emily's booming voice once again. 'The dish is cracked!' she shouted, and snatched the serving spoon out of Cissy's hand. She whacked the cabbage dish. There was a telltale clank of cracked china. 'I knew it,' she cried and hurled the spoon across the table, straight at me.

I ducked. The spoon sailed past me and bounced on the carpet behind my chair. I had barely turned around again when Emily's blue-veined old hands reached for the dish and wrenched it away from Cissy.

This time it was the dish that came flying through the air. It exploded against the wall, leaving a cascade of broken china and limp cabbage. Rivulets of pale, watery green poured down the wall and formed a pool on the Indian rug.

'Belovèd would never have allowed a *cracked* dish,' she bellowed. Everyone stared in stunned silence. Some of the old ladies were open-mouthed. I could see their half-chewed food.

'What happened?' enquired 86-year-old Toto, one of my favourite old ladies, but near-sighted to the point of blindness. She turned her head from side to side in an effort to focus on the disturbance, looking just like Gay when she sniffed the wind.

No one answered. Then suddenly Emily was surrounded by old ladies. 'There, there,' comforted one. 'I know, I know,' muttered another. 'Going senile, I shouldn't wonder,' pronounced Olive, as Emily was led muttering from the dining room and the mess hastily wiped up.

Margaret and I giggled over the incident that afternoon with Ann, but I had to wait until bedtime when Waa was tucking me in for an explanation. 'Why did Emily throw the dish, Waa?' I asked.

'She was cross about the dish being cracked. She's an old lady, Kitty.'

'Did she get into trouble?'

'No, Kitty, she didn't. Everyone understands.'

'I don't.'

Waa stopped tucking me in and sat on the edge of the bed. 'You would have to have known your grandfather, Kitty, to really understand,' she said, stroking my hair. 'Everything seemed possible when Dear Belovèd was alive. He was such a wonderful man, you just wanted to always do your very best, every hour of every day. I think what upset Emily today was a cracked dish being used. It would never have happened in Belovèd's day, not because he would have been cross but because even the slightest imperfection was unthinkable . . .'

'But—' I began.

'Shhh,' she soothed. 'You'll understand. One day.'

* * *

It was to be many years before I understood what Waa meant, but within a few weeks of arriving to live in the 'Agapemone' – a Greek word, my sisters informed me, that means 'abode of love' – I had divined the way my strange new home worked, in the way that young children often instinctively can. I had liked it immediately: its vast, mostly unkempt gardens, more than 20 bedrooms, central heating and its chapel, known simply as Eden. Plenty of room for my mother, my two older sisters and me, plus our 79-year-old nanny. Soon I learned not to fear the very old ladies who inched their way around dressed in fashions the like of which I had only seen in history books.

This shabby yet luxurious mansion in Spaxton, Somerset, was, I soon decided, much nicer than the draughty, spider-infested houses we had rented in nearby villages since my parents' marriage had collapsed following my father's return from Germany, where he had been detained in a prisoner-of-war camp. I had only ever seen my father once and my parents had never owned their own house. Perhaps he never understood that my mother had believed that when they married she had put her strange background behind her. To return home, her marriage in tatters, meant she had failed both in her marriage and in her escape.

And, already a veteran of my small, loving boarding school (I had been sent there aged five, the previous year), I found comfort in the institutional order of my new home: the bells which summoned the faithful to meals; the obligatory post-luncheon 'quiet time', which resulted in hours of unsupervised freedom for us children; the elderly members of the 'Kitchen Parlour' ready to cater to my every want.

I stopped being afraid of my fierce grandmother, who ruled from her wing in the east end of the mansion. Autocratic and above the daily comings and goings of the community, she rarely even ventured beyond the baize door which marked the wing of the mansion still referred to as 'Belovèd's End'.

I soon learned – even if I failed to understand – that next to her in precedence within the community came my mother, Lavita, then thirty-eight, and her two older brothers, David and Patrick. Patrick didn't live with us but visited daily from his own home some miles away. David, the eldest and an officer in the Merchant Navy, was often away at sea.

I grew to love David. I sometimes even secretly wished he was my father. When he arrived home on shore leave, sometimes in his uniform and driving a Rolls-Royce, or some other luxurious car he always rented, I could have burst with pride. I never tired of listening to my mother tell of how brave he had been during the war when he was on the North Atlantic running the gauntlet of U-boats in an unarmed merchant ship. My mother later told me that, ironically, his most serious injuries were sustained when he was attacked by two South African soldiers in London while on leave. She explained that Merchant Navy officers didn't wear uniform while off duty, and the two assailants probably hadn't realised he was serving his country.

I thought the silk hanky he always tucked into his shirt cuff very dashing and loved the smell of his cologne. He had learnt to play the piano before the war and had also studied at the Sorbonne. He would tell me of his days in Paris in the 1930s, where he had mixed with Elizabeth David, the famous cookery-book author, and Josephine

Baker, the black jazz singer. He was very proud to have been personal assistant to the 7th Earl Beauchamp, who had served as governor of New South Wales in Australia and warden of the Cinque Ports until his resignation in 1931 following his 'outing' as a homosexual. My uncle had been at the earl's bedside when he had died in New York seven years later.

Uncle David's most important quality, however, as far as I was concerned, was his kindness towards our mother, especially now that she was divorced. Even though somewhere he had an ex-wife and a daughter, his sister came first in his heart and he never failed to bring her a present each time he came home. He wrote to her frequently and, whenever possible, paid for her to visit him in one of the ports he stayed in on leave for weeks at a time.

But where my feelings for Uncle David were uncomplicated, it was a different matter with his younger brother – referred to as 'Panion' by the old ladies (when he was born, he was deemed to be a com*panion* to his older brother). He could be charming, and often was when he wasn't drinking. Then he was fun to be around, with his stories of the racecourse and market day; letting me handle the ferrets that he kept in cages at his home and his pet dogs, which he would exercise by making them run after his vehicle. But it took very little for his handsome features to suddenly become suffused with fury and his cursing to send me running. What was he so angry and frustrated about? As a child, I hadn't a clue. I understand better now how his strange upbringing had left him a confused and frustrated man. Yet I loved the aura of energy that filled any room he was in and I tried to imitate his constant tuneless whistle, which would start my grandmother muttering, 'Empty vessels make most sound.'

Uncle Pat was always immaculately turned out, mostly in breeches, with gaiters shiny enough that I could see my face in them, and trilby hats, which gave him a decidedly gentrified appearance. There also clung to him the faintest aroma of the stableyard, one even more pronounced on market days when his clothes were redolent with the smells of the town's local livestock market and the numerous public houses he frequented. I never remember his holding down a job – except for a brief spell on a factory production line – but he seemed to live in comfort with his wife 'Babe', a local farmer's daughter, and their growing family in a house in a nearby village given to him by my grandmother. He was never short of cash, always appearing to have enough to deal in pigs and other livestock – and be well known in local betting and racing circles. He spent most afternoons barking instructions to his bookmaker over the phone in my grandmother's downstairs drawing room, which used to be my grandfather's study.

Uncle Pat also had the most beautiful copperplate handwriting, which I again unsuccessfully tried to copy, although even at six I could spell much better than him. Waa explained to me how he had wanted to be a farmer or an auctioneer, but that my grandmother had 'put her foot down'. Grandmother couldn't stop him dealing in livestock, but it just would not have done to have had a member of the 'Holy Family' working as a farm labourer. In the 1950s he was to spend many months in a sanatorium, recovering from tuberculosis.

Years later, during a particularly difficult time for my Aunt Babe, she told me how, as a young man, Pat had worked for her father, who had become concerned that his daughter might be falling for the handsome young man. 'Don't marry him,' he had cautioned her. When she asked her father why not, he told her it wasn't that he didn't like the young man – he did – 'But he won't make you happy,' he'd said.

On special occasions, or when she decreed, my grandmother would invite us children to take tea with her in her upstairs boudoir which overlooked the small, square garden bound by Eden, the estate wall and my favourite hiding place, the huge blue cedar bordering the long driveway to the front door. It was a shaded room, full of light and with that secure atmosphere which children love. It was filled with graceful Edwardian furniture, so was different from the rest of the mansion with its ornate Victorian contents. My favourite piece in the room was the tall corner cupboard filled with intriguing objects: pieces of delicate porcelain, and tiny wooden and ivory carved animals, all souvenirs of her and my grandfather's travels in Europe and Scandinavia.

Granny's Windsor armchair was always drawn close to the fireplace, which boasted a glowing wood flame on all but the very hottest days. An old-fashioned radio stood on a nearby table. Sometimes we would be allowed to sit with Granny after lunch and listen to programmes on the wireless while she dozed on the chaise longue. Other times, she would tell me stories about her childhood and the days before she met grandfather. I never once remember hearing her refer to him as Belovèd, and it would be years before I learned that the name – or, perhaps more accurately, his title – was taken from the Song of Solomon.

I was always expected to arrive exactly five minutes early for tea to help Granny hunt for her false teeth, which she regularly removed for her rest and just as regularly misplaced. Yet she made a regal figure in her blue chiffon veil and with her ramrod straight back. Years later I would learn that outsiders assumed her veil to be some kind of bizarre badge of office. My mother maintained it was nothing of the sort, just that my grandmother had suffered a severe ear infection as a young woman and wore the veil to protect her 'delicate ears'.

By the time my sisters and I came to live at the Agapemone, she was also blind and suffering from cancer of the nose, which left a raw wound that had to be dressed daily by a visiting nurse. But none of her very real afflictions daunted her, and she dominated the household and her children until the day she died.

In the early days, I didn't give much thought to the old ladies, except that there seemed to be a lot of them and that they obviously were of lower status than my grandmother, mother and uncles – and, to a lesser extent, us three. We were loved by the old ladies in a Victorian 'children must be seen and not heard' fashion and supervised by our nanny. I certainly had no idea they were the survivors of a band of followers who had been led by my grandfather and his predecessor, and who, having donated their personal fortunes on joining the community, had been rewarded for their generosity with a life of ease.

At the time, I didn't realise just what highly gifted women they were. They had no doubt been ostracised as 'eccentric' by mainstream Victorian and Edwardian society, but here, in this weirdly emancipated community, they flourished. Violet Morris was still busy designing houses: the latest, at the far end of the village, was one of many examples of her talent in and around Spaxton. Her sister Olive, a self-taught engineer and woodcarver, had learned to drive in the early 1900s and still spent her days in her workshop, knee deep in shavings. Examples of her carvings appeared everywhere and were proudly pointed out to me; one day I would learn they filled not only the community but the London Ark of the Covenant as well. The two sisters lived in one of the three 'gates', large comfortable houses built at the northern, western and eastern points of the estate.

Some of the other ladies were renegades from the wealthy Victorian merchant class, like Ada Kemp, of the Kemp biscuit family. Toto, whose real name was Phoebe Ker, was the daughter of a wealthy merchant who had paid the printing costs for *Voice of the Bride*, the community hymnal once used in the chapel and the London church. Her brother was a publisher in America and her niece, Grace, made regular, lengthy visits to Spaxton following her retirement as headmistress of a girls' school on Long Island, New York. Time and again it would be myopic Toto who would sense emotional distress and come to the rescue of those caught up in the legacy of our grandfather's outrageous claim.

Waa had told us that she herself was a Wiltshire country girl who, until leaving to help our mother with us, had spent her entire adult life in the community after her brothers had been killed in various Empire wars. She told us how 'Dear Belovèd', our grandfather, had appointed her nanny to my uncles and mother when they were born and, in turn, she had cared for us. She also loved to relate stories of her Wiltshire childhood, playing cricket with her brothers and spotting fireflies at dusk, and she told us that her name was Margaret Davis, but that her father and brothers had taken to calling her Fanny; her nickname, Waa, had come about when David, as a baby, had been unable to say Margaret. Waa sewed our school uniforms on an ancient Singer sewing machine she kept in her tiny bedroom. She made the scrumptious egg sandwiches we carried when we went fox-hunting, and packed them in immaculate greaseproof-paper parcels, complete with 'hospital corners' and white string tied in a bow. She read us stories every bedtime and wrote us our weekly letters from home when we were away at boarding school, always concluding with the phrase, 'Mummy sends her love.'

As an old-fashioned 'nanny', she did her best to ensure we were protected from our mother's continuing battle with alcohol. I only realised just what a battle it was for my mother in my teenage years when I began to appreciate her circumstances. How ironic that the strange concept of freedom my grandfather's female followers had embraced was to result in my mother's imprisonment in this 'paradise'.

Waa was also a loving influence in helping me overcome a severe bedwetting problem, which started shortly after I was sent to boarding school. She never took me to task, merely reassuring me every morning I woke in a soaking bed that this was a very temporary situation which would end as suddenly as it had begun. And, of course, it did – but not completely until I had put both boarding school and the Agapemone behind me.

Initially, Ann, Margaret and I didn't know each other as well as I imagine most sisters do. This was partly as a result of our age difference: Ann is seven years older than me and Margaret is five years my elder. We also attended different boarding schools. The main reason, however, for our emotional distance as children was that it had been well into 1942 before I had even met my sisters. I was born in Egypt, where our mother had followed her army officer husband during the early years of the Second World War, leaving my sisters in England in the care of my grandmother and Waa. I was a toddler by the time I met Ann and Margaret, and they've told me their biggest worry at my arrival had been that I would steal all their toys!

Catering to the motley collection of individuals who made up the Agapemone was another set of old ladies known as the 'Kitchen Parlour' – so-called after the gloomy room off the kitchens where they took their meals, exactly one hour before the rest of us. This was also where they rested after their day's labour, and woe betide us if we entered uninvited. Believers like their more wealthy fellow members but lacking worldly wealth, they had instead given a lifetime of labour. The word 'servant' was never used to describe this ever-diminishing group of elderly women; they were simply the KP. In addition to their serving duties, Lettit and Cissy ran the community laundry from a long, low building filled with Victorian wash tubs, mangles and serried ranks of irons.

It was a magical place to call home. We were not only warmed by central heating that flourished as efficiently as it surely had half a century before but by the welcome shown us by the old ladies, who daily inched their way around the huge mansion. We were, after all, Dear Belovèd's granddaughters. It would take me a long time to realise that the old ladies I lived with were sometimes overcome with sadness and perhaps even regret. But by the time I was mature enough to understand this, I was consumed with questions of my own.

2

&

The Beginning

We all knew our new home was 'different' – the world beyond those high stone walls never let us forget it – but just how different and the reasons why would take many years to unearth. I first learned the genesis of the Agapemone from *The Abode of Love*, a novel based on my childhood home by English satirist Aubrey Menen. I was 17, and the family who had employed me briefly as their au pair lent it to me. Neither the job nor the book were enjoyable experiences, but the revelations contained in that slim volume did contribute to my quest at the time.

* * *

It all began in the 1840s. England was emerging from 70 turbulent years of sweeping change, moving from an agrarian society to an intensely industrial one. The Industrial Revolution had loosened the shackles of feudalism expressed in Cecil Frances Alexander's famous hymn 'All things bright and beautiful', written in 1848:

> *The rich man at his castle,*
> *The poor man at his gate,*
> *God made them high and mighty,*
> *He ordered their estate.*

Wealth, once the domain of the noble born, was becoming more accessible to the merchant class. But, at the other end of the economic scale, a whole new level of poverty was emerging as country folk abandoned their villages in increasing numbers to work in urban factories. The resulting dislocation, economic change and appalling working conditions produced waves of protest and began to strain the already shaky moral and religious fibres of this island nation.

It must have seemed a bewildering new world. The abolition of slavery was being talked about at a conference in London. The kingdom's new young queen, Victoria, was marrying a foreigner. *The Old Curiosity Shop* by Charles Dickens, 'sympathizer to the poor, the suffering, and the oppressed', was about to be published on the heels of *Oliver Twist*, the masterpiece that had drawn attention to an endemic cruelty to children. And, unremarked upon by the great chroniclers of the day, a charismatic young Anglican curate, fresh from his examinations and a turbulent college career, set off for Somerset to take up a curacy in the tiny village of Charlinch, next door to Spaxton.

Agapemone founder Reverend Henry James Prince had originally set his sights on the medical profession and held down a post in a Bath hospital before illness forced him to give up his career in favour of the Church. His widowed mother had been appalled at his career change, not because she had anything against clergymen – they were very necessary, in their way, and far more socially acceptable than mere physicians – but because she disapproved of what she considered her young son's unhealthy relationship with her lodger. Martha Freeman, the daughter of a West Indian planter, was a wealthy spinster, a devout Roman Catholic and more than twice Henry's age.

The besotted Martha paid for young Henry's theological training at St David's College in Lampeter, Wales. This new foundation, set up to stem the turbulent waters of religious nonconformity threatening the established Church at the time, sent its graduates forth to win back dissenters. Mainstream Christianity was no longer as satisfying as it had once been; people from all walks of life were questioning their beliefs and searching for a more meaningful spiritual path. Christian evangelism was becoming more popular in England and the United States, where utopian sects such as the Mormons, Adventists and the Christadelphians were all soon to establish themselves. But the principal and faculty of St David's College were strictly old school, drawn from the ranks of noble younger sons, witty with an easy superiority and a decidedly Georgian view of religion. Most had a taste for riding to hounds and vintage claret, fine sherry and old port. These worldly clergymen disliked – maybe even feared – any movement that could upset their pleasant social order.

Twenty-six-year-old Henry was appalled by his superiors. He was also disgusted by the laissez-faire attitude of most of his fellow students to their calling. He decided to show them the error of their ways and formed a group of like-minded zealots. These 'Lampeter Brethren' set about their self-appointed task with a will, interrupting services with their abrasive fervour – on one occasion he and his followers angrily stalked out of the vice-principal's cocktail party to hoots of derision from their more worldly fellow students, who saw nothing wrong in the pleasant social life of a country vicar.

Yet the college authorities could do little about these troublesome Lampeter Brethren. Prince and his followers continued to excel in their studies, making it impossible to send them down. And when he wasn't fighting the faculty, Prince was writing long, rambling letters to his beloved Martha back in Bath. During his holidays the two closeted themselves in her room where Henry would woo her with verses from the Bible's erotic Song of Solomon. To the devout young student, the book's language, especially when recited aloud, must surely have appealed to his awakening sensuality, as well as his love of the written word – he would prove a gifted writer and eventually produce a huge volume of religious tracts and pamphlets. On a deeper level still, Henry's belief that the book's underlying message was that the Church was the bride of Christ appealed to his growing religious obsession and would form the basis of his strange beliefs.

But as she anxiously paced the floor downstairs, his mother was only concerned with what she believed was her son's obsession with this much older woman.

In July 1838, the ill-matched pair married. But Martha's young husband insisted their marriage be 'in spirit' only; there could be no carnal relations. Prince then returned to St David's to complete his studies. Two long years later – no doubt for Martha as well as the college faculty – Henry graduated and was given a curacy in Charlinch. When the young curate and his adoring wife arrived in this bucolic corner of England, they found the congregation anything but God-fearing, and the parish's wealthy and well-born incumbent absent. The Reverend Samuel Starky had taken himself off to die on the Isle of Wight.

Prince set about reclaiming the lost souls of Charlinch, preaching long and fiery sermons filled with hellfire and damnation. A year later his proselytising still hadn't cut any ice with his congregation, who continued to choose the local public house over church pews, perhaps wary of this new religious call to arms.

Prince's elderly wife returned to Bath, very probably disillusioned with her 'spiritual' marriage and no doubt worn out with the struggle to claim the hearts and minds of an obdurate congregation. Memories are long in the countryside, and perhaps in Prince's fiery promises of paradise these farmers, farriers and labourers heard echoes of what had happened a century and a half before, when they flocked to the Protestant losing side in the Duke of Monmouth's disastrous insurrection against the Catholic King James.

Far away on the Isle of Wight the parish incumbent, still reclining on what he had convinced himself was to be his deathbed, received a printed copy of one of his curate's sermons. He would later claim the words jolted him back to health. As soon as he was well enough, Starky returned to Charlinch and, unlike his congregation, fell under Prince's spell, believing his curate's prediction that the end of history was nigh and only those who believed would find salvation in an earthly paradise.

One Sunday in October 1841, Starky, so consumed by his curate's predictions, mounted the pulpit to deliver his customary sermon. Silence! He tried again. He waved his arms. He groaned. He muttered. His tiny congregation looked on in concern. Was their parson ill? After several more minutes of inexplicable gesticulating Starky stepped down from the pulpit, leaving his curate to explain that the Holy Ghost had deserted his religious superior. The following Sunday several dozen curious worshippers showed up at the church door. Once again, Starky appeared to be struck dumb.

Within a month the place was packed, as news of the 'mad parson' spread across the county. So was the local public house. After each increasingly bizarre service the congregation would dash down the steep hill to the Lamb Inn in the neighbouring village of Spaxton, where they would quench their thirst on draughts of powerful scrumpy cider and fight with the pub's resentful regulars.

It took a month for the Holy Ghost to return to the Reverend Starky – a month in which Prince and a small coterie of followers prayed daily that the parson's voice be restored. And then one Sunday in November, as an expectant hush had fallen over the packed pews, Starky mounted the steps to the pulpit and began to preach, miraculously in full voice. Prince was later to claim the sermon Starky delivered that evening was 'searching as fire, heavy as a hammer, sharper than a two-edged sword', and that the return of his superior's voice was a miracle, implying, of course, that he'd had a hand in it.

It was just what was needed. Soon Charlinch had become the centre of a noisy religious revival. People flocked to the church in ever-increasing numbers. Prayer groups and ladies' groups were formed. Children attending Sunday School wailed in distress at their own wickedness. Chaos reigned. Members of the Lampeter Brethren were called on to help trumpet Prince's message that the end of history would be marked by an earthly paradise for the saved. He went one step further and decided to separate the wheat – those he deemed truly possessed of the spirit – from the chaff – those he suspected attended out of curiosity. This 'chaff' did not like their label, especially as many of them were prosperous farmers and considered themselves important in village life. When these 'sinners' discovered that their vicar intended to literally bar them from attending church services – as well as entering the gates of paradise – they were scandalised.

Once again, the countryside erupted in such turmoil that even the elderly and indolent Bishop of Bath and Wells could no longer ignore the effect Starky and Prince were having on the locals. Starky was summoned to the bishop's palace in the tranquil cathedral city of Wells and told to get rid of his mad curate.

Starky told Prince about the bishop's edict, and Prince ignored it. But an unusual calm did descend on the parish for a couple of weeks, mainly because Prince had been summoned to Bath following his wife's death. He didn't mourn for long and within weeks had married Reverend Starky's sister Julia. She too was much older than him and was also told the marriage would be a spiritual one.

Prince returned to saving souls in Charlinch, especially female ones, the younger and prettier the better, it seemed. Soon husbands and fathers grew uneasy. The bishop was approached again and decided to revoke Prince's licence to preach in the diocese.

The young curate appeared unconcerned, but the reason for his behaviour was soon evident: William Cobbe, a wealthy engineer who had worked with famous Victorian engineer Isambard Kingdom Brunel, had given Prince a parcel of land in nearby Spaxton and would design and build Prince's earthly paradise.

One hundred years later, this earthly paradise would become my childhood home.

3

An Invitation

Esther Ann Walter died, aged 95.

Entry in the Agapemone diary on
Saturday, 19 March 1949

Margaret had already made it to the apex of the roof above Granny's quarters in the east end of the mansion. Her thick hair falling across her face, she looked as at ease clinging on to the ridge as if she were leaning over a gate, thanks to her astonishing head for heights – much like her courage. All of us were by now decent riders, but Margaret could quiet the most temperamental horse. And in her tree- and roof-climbing she had no equal.

'Come on, Kitty!' she called. 'There's nothing to worry about.'

I started up the steep roof, sandals gripping the slates. On reaching her, I too looked over and then, to prove how brave I was, sat astride the roof, gripping the cold slates between my legs. What if I slipped? I imagined tumbling down, arms and legs flailing, as I tried to stop myself, Margaret's hands reaching out to grab me, eyes wide and her face a mask of horror.

But Margaret had already started back down.

'Hurry up, Kitty. Someone will see you,' she urged.

I glanced down past the attic window we had climbed out of, to where my sister crouched in the valley between the mansion's roofs and was proceeding to lay out the draughts board. Beyond her, framed in the V-shaped gap, were the cottages, once home to most of the Kitchen Parlour but now almost empty as their former occupants passed away or moved into the warmth of the main house. Looking back over my shoulder, I could see a deckchair that had been left outside Granny's bathroom all night on the 'leads' (the balcony area made of lead) – trouble for Ellen if Granny found out! I realised I had never before been level with the huge stone lion rampant which stood at the farthest end of the chapel roof, holding a peeling flagpole in its giant paws. Waa had told me it used to fly a huge flag of a lion lying with a lamb on a bed of lilies but that it hadn't been raised since my grandfather died.

'Why doesn't anybody use Eden, Margaret?' I called from my perch.

'Because Grandfather is dead.'

'But everyone dies – look at Esther – and they don't just stop using churches.' Far away in the distance I caught sight of the top of the daily bus from Bridgwater crawling between the hedges. 'I can see the bus.'

'Then they can see you,' she replied. 'If we get caught up here, we'll be in trouble.'

I forced myself to look down, all the way to the ground and Granny's small garden. My stomach lurched and my feet tingled as I focused on the blackbird sipping at the birdbath in the centre of the lawn. Turning away, I started back down to join my sister, using my sandals as brakes.

'We probably won't have time to go rooting [which we pronounced *rowting*] before everyone wakes up,' Margaret announced as I settled opposite her. 'Especially as the doctor is coming to certify Esther's dead.' I shivered. The thought of someone lying dead in one of the rooms still gave me the creeps. I would grow used to it.

'But you promised,' I whined. We used the word rooting to mean nosing around wherever our curiosity took us. It meant we could arrange trips to the empty rooms without the others knowing.

Distracted, I looked at the pieces Margaret had laid out on the draughtboard. 'You've got white.' Margaret always took white, another disadvantage of being the baby of the family. 'And you've already moved.'

'I had to start if you want to go rooting.'

'But I wasn't here.'

'Shh, Kitty. Someone will hear.'

I lost. We had already started a second game when I felt something land on my head. I looked up in surprise, just in time for a huge drop of water to land in one eye.

'Come on, before the roof gets slippery,' Margaret commanded. Sweeping the pieces into the box, she tucked it under her arm and started back up the roof to the attic window. I scrambled after her, my sandals starting to slip as I reached for the frame. A loose slate rattled past me, breaking as it hit the guttering.

'For goodness' sake,' hissed Margaret from inside the attic bedroom.

She closed the window, carefully wiping our wet footprints from the sill. We were in one of a suite of small, sloped-ceiling attic rooms above Granny's end. Once occupied by our grandparents' personal staff, most of the furniture had long been disposed of. Even I had carried away a small rocking chair to my latest bedroom.

All that remained in the little attic room was a small Davenport desk which I was sure would be unlikely to offer worthwhile rooting. I wanted a room filled with furniture, containing the relics of the bygone age we were used to unearthing. So far, we had collected a brass microscope, Wedgwood dressing-table sets, birds' eggs (including an ostrich egg) and carefully labelled fossils by the dozen picked up along the Dorset coast. We took anything we could use, although what we thought we could do with a pair of ivory glove stretchers, I'm not sure.

'Why are you pouting, Kitty?' Margaret asked, as I stared around the bare little room.

'There's nothing here.'

'That's where you're wrong.' She tugged at a little door I hadn't noticed tucked into the wall below the window. It swung open and Margaret disappeared into the darkness on all-fours. I followed.

At first, it was so dark I could see nothing. Then Margaret pulled a chain hanging from the ceiling and I found myself surrounded by dolls: ones with blue eyes and brown eyes, and eyes with long lashes or no lashes at all. I had never seen so many, and all of them were dressed in old-fashioned clothes, some even carrying parasols. And not just dolls – an old teddy bear sat in a tiny wicker pram and a doll's house stood in the corner with its front half-open, showing tiny rooms full of tiny furniture, down to a set of saucepans on the kitchen stove and the tiniest umbrella stand I had ever seen. In another corner were an old wooden fire engine, some model cars, a train set, a tricycle and boxes of games, and beyond them all what looked like a pile of photo albums.

Margaret reached for the nearest doll, tipping it backwards until its long black eyelashes rested on its china cheeks. 'Welcome to Jericho,' she squeaked. For as long as my sisters could remember, this cupboard had been called Jericho – heaven knows why. She lifted the doll's long, lace-trimmed skirt to reveal ankle-length lacy knickers. 'This was Uncle David's favourite doll.' She gestured at the others. 'They were all his.'

'Men don't play with dolls.'

'He did when he was a boy. Waa told me.'

I didn't believe her, but I wanted to play with the doll's house too much to argue. There was something about its tiny perfect world that appealed to me: just two bedrooms, a bathroom, a kitchen, sitting room and dining room. I crouched and squinted through half-closed eyes to make it more real, picturing the door at the back of the kitchen opening and my father coming in with an armful of vegetables he had just picked from the garden. I had no memory of my father. I had only met him once, when I was four years old, and his features had faded. I had to rely on what I had been told, that he was tall, dark and handsome. Then I imagined Mummy – no, it would be Waa – at the stove, for our mother could barely boil an egg. I saw myself polishing the silver and setting the table for lunch in the dining room. As we would be an ordinary family, we would only need six places, not the dozen or more I knew at home.

I was so caught up in my fantasy that I almost yelled when Margaret poked me hard in the back. 'Someone's coming,' she hissed, pulling on the chain and door simultaneously, plunging us into sudden darkness.

We heard the bedroom door squeak and footsteps coming in our direction. Light flooded our hiding place as the cupboard door was flung open. It was Ann, grinning, and with her brown eyes all sparkly. I was very proud of my soon-to-be-15-year-old sister, who was so grown up she even wore a brassiere – unlike Margaret, who still had pimples for bosoms.

'You might have said it was you,' Margaret complained.

'Sorry.' Ann pulled the door wider. 'Come on out – not you, Kitty – I have got something to tell you, Margaret.'

I was delighted, wanting to cling to my fantasy a little while longer.

'You can't stay in there, Kitty, on your own,' Ann hesitated. 'You might break something.'

'I won't, I promise.'

To my amazement, Ann relented. 'Just for a minute.' She even reached in and pulled the light on for me before shutting the door. I knew from experience that this meant she had something to tell Margaret that was worth listening to. I put my ear to the door.

'He's asked me out, Margaret.'

'When?'

'Tomorrow.'

'Where?'

'His mother is giving a party and he's asked me.'

'Gosh!'

A boy! How boring! I turned back to the doll's house.

* * *

Later that same day, the three of us met for a cup of tea in the pantry used by Ellen, the member of the Kitchen Parlour who catered to our grandmother's every want. She sometimes allowed us to make tea in her domain, and today was one of those occasions, because she was busy laying out Esther, who had just died. We were just helping ourselves to a couple of arrowroot biscuits – I don't remember there ever being any other kind of afternoon biscuit served, and at least these ones were fresh, which was a pleasant surprise – when Waa hurried in.

'There's a young man on the telephone for you, Ann,' she said.

Even Margaret looked impressed. No one ever telephoned us. And we didn't know any boys – at least I didn't. Ann blushed and ran from the room. I stifled a giggle.

Waa had barely poured herself a cup of tea and settled on one of the hard chairs when Ann was back. I could tell at once something was wrong. Her eyes had lost their sparkle and she had a bright angry blush to her cheeks. 'I'm not going,' she blurted out to her sister. 'He said he was sorry, but his mother told him I couldn't.' Ann rarely cried, so I was horrified – and puzzled as to why this was such a big deal – when she began to gulp back sobs. 'She says our family is too peculiar.'

Margaret slammed her empty teacup back in its saucer. 'That's so unfair.'

'Just because we live in a big house,' I added, not wanting to be left out.

'Don't be stupid, Kitty,' Ann shouted.

'You don't know anything,' added Margaret.

'Now, children,' Waa intervened. 'If someone is going to be so unkind, Ann, then all I can say is they're not worth knowing.'

Ann ran from the room, slamming the door so hard she made the cups and saucers rattle. Margaret followed her. I sat there, confused.

'Waa, why does that boy's mother say our family is peculiar?'

'It's not, dear.'

'Then why did that boy's mother say it was? Is it because Mummy is divorced?'

'Bless your soul, no,' Waa smiled and reached across to pat my hand. 'But there have always been people who don't understand, even in your grandfather's day.'

'What don't they understand?'

'What a great and wonderful man your grandfather was. How he was right about so many things.'

It was an unsatisfactory answer, the first of many. School soon beckoned, though, and I was caught up in my busy life there, where I relegated my unspoken questions to the recesses of my young mind.

* * *

When I returned home for Easter, I found plans had been made for Margaret and me to go and stay with our paternal grandparents in their Cornwall home during our summer holidays. I was excited about the train journey, during which we would travel under the watchful eyes of the guard, but apprehensive about staying with people I barely knew, even if they were my grandparents.

From the first moment I set eyes on their stone house set in a large and cared-for garden, I loved Glenview. Grandpa John was a tall, balding man with a ready smile and given to reducing me to helpless laughter with his habit of popping whole jam tarts in his mouth, to the mock disgust of my grandmother. Granny May was a revelation – I had never dreamed I had such a bustling, competent relative as she, who could turn out delicious meals in what, in my limited experience, was a tiny kitchen. She seemed a friendly, no-nonsense woman with glittering black eyes who appeared to know us all much better than I imagined. As did her spinster sister, Great Aunt Tup, who was a matron of a girls' boarding school but was staying at Glenview during the holidays.

Granny May asked after 'Ruth', which, to me, seemed overly familiar. After all, she couldn't know her very well and surely she didn't imagine I ever thought of my exacting grandmother as merely 'Ruth'. Granny May also spoke of my mother and her brothers, not unkindly but without affection. Her implied criticisms of Waa shocked me – my elderly nanny was above reproach, as far as I was concerned. And I puzzled over her enigmatic comments about the 'Read silver', which our family apparently still possessed. And her muttered asides to Grandpa John: 'Of course, the "incident" was entirely responsible for your father's early death,' she had said. Grandpa John made some noncommittal reply and the subject was hastily changed.

Later, I asked Margaret what the 'incident' was. She shrugged. 'I have no idea. But it will be all our family's fault, whatever it is.'

In general, I enjoyed myself. I found the days too full of fun to anguish over such adult concerns and I grew to love the spacious old house and its rambling garden. And what a revelation to get to know our youngest uncle, my grandparents' youngest son, Stephen, who was just two years older than my eldest sister. To me, he seemed like a young god – until I woke him up one day by tipping a glass of water over his face. He yelped and flung up a hand, sending the glass flying. It hit my eyebrow. Blood joined the river of water and stitches at the local hospital resulted.

Soon, the two weeks were over and Margaret and I made the return journey to our Somerset home.

* * *

Summer had come and gone, and I had endured the painful return to boarding school. But, as always, within a couple of weeks I had settled down. I was mildly surprised when the first of my weekends home came around. On this occasion I was on my own, as my sisters were not due until the following weekend. After breakfast the next morning I went to say good morning to my mother and Uncle David.

'She's an ungrateful wretch,' I heard Uncle David shout from beyond the study door.

I stopped, wondering what I had done. Mummy's reply was muffled, but I made out the word 'Ann'. I leaned closer and learned Ann had written from boarding school to say that next year, when she was 16 and had the right to choose with whom she lived, she intended to stay with Daddy.

My heart sank. She had always said she would leave home as soon as she finished school, which would be when she was 17. This I could accept, because it was what you did. But to lose her sooner, to our father, who was in the army, raised the possibility I might never see her again. And if she went, Margaret might too, and then I truly would be on my own. (She didn't, but I had no way of knowing that then.)

I turned away, fighting tears. Determined not to be seen crying, I wandered out to the conservatory by the kitchens and spent half an hour watching our gardener, Edward, tend to the forest of tomato plants which would soon blossom with huge, round fruit, filling the glass building with their heady aroma. Then it was but a few yards to the community laundry, a pair of small, low-ceilinged cottages reached by the path that led from the back of the conservatory. The laundry's back door stood ajar.

'Don't you think so, Cissy?' I heard Lettit say.

I pushed the door wider. Lettit was feeding a sheet rhythmically between the rollers of a hand-turned mangle, her words punctuating the whoosh of water into the waiting bucket. When she saw me, she straightened, pushed back her straggly grey hair and then lifted the sheet into a big oval basket, ready for the line.

'We have a visitor, Cissy, dear,' she called, smiling a welcome. 'I do declare you've grown an inch since you went back to school,' she said in her lilting Welsh accent.

Cissy poked her head around the door, a little old goblin with white curls. In one hand she held a freshly heated heavy black iron. 'You're shooting up, dear, just like your sisters. The food must be very good at your boarding school.' Cissy turned and spat on the iron, sending beads of saliva skittering. Satisfied, she carried the iron across the room to the huge ironing board and the pile of damp, rolled-up table napkins.

I wrinkled my nose. 'Except for the meat.' It wasn't done to say you liked school food, which was, in fact, very good.

'So, to what do we owe this honour? On your first day home too.' Cissy's gnarled old fingers smoothed the first napkin. A few swipes with the iron, four folds, another finishing swipe and it was finished, the copperplate writing sitting in one corner so it could be seen easily. All the linen, even the bed sheets, was marked 'Agapemone', with an ornate A in indelible ink and underneath to where it should be returned: Belovèd's End, Dining Room, West End, East Gate etc. 'A young lady like you must have much more interesting things to do than talk to two old ladies like us,' she went on.

I stuffed my hands deep in the pockets of my jodhpurs. I could keep the terrible information to myself no longer. 'Ann wants to go and live with our father,' I burst out.

'Well, I never!' Lettit paused in her mangling and crossed to sit in one of the two upright chairs by the window, overlooking the road. 'You'll miss her, and so will dear Margaret.'

'And so will poor Lavita,' added Cissy.

I hadn't given much thought to how Mummy would feel. But I had noticed how hunched and sad she always looked when Uncle David was away at sea. Now, I wondered, did she look like that when we were at school? Would she look like that all the time if my oldest sister went to live with our father? Would the empty days and solitary evenings with only whisky and a detective novel from the Boots library for company seem even longer?

'Why does Ann want to live with her father, Kitty?' Cissy went to reheat the iron on the hob and joined her sister by the window.

I shrugged, reluctant to tell the old ladies about the boyfriend's mother who had called our family 'peculiar'. Repeating it only seemed to make the puzzling accusation more likely to be true. And I still had no idea why. Although there had been other incidents, like the time Ann and Margaret had gone to a hunt ball at the Pony Club. They had both returned home mortified. Everyone else had been in 'a crowd' and they had had to sit on their own at dinner. Then someone had taken pity on them and tried to be kind by asking if they would like to join their party. It had been even worse than being ignored, they'd said.

'Dear Polo,' Lettit sighed. 'Such a nice boy, he always was.'

Dear Polo? How did Lettit and Cissy know my father?

'By far the best looking of May's boys,' Cissy twinkled at her sister. 'You know, Lettit, I wasn't the least bit surprised when—'

'You know our father? Leopold John Douglas Read?'

The two little old ladies looked at each other the way grown-ups do when they realise they have let a cat out of the bag. 'We haven't seen him for years,' explained Lettit, 'but when they were boys, we saw lots of Polo – that's what he was always called – and his brothers. He was number two of the four.' She pointed at an angle through the small window. 'He was born in Home Cottage, round the corner and next door to the post office. Now, Stephen – number five – we never knew because he was born long after the others. Wasn't that so, Cissy? Do I recall correctly?'

'You knew Granny May?' Suddenly Granny May's knowledge of my home made sense.

'Why, yes, dear.' Cissy smoothed her apron with her rickety, bent fingers.

'She used to live here when she was a young woman. And this is where she met your grandfather – your father's father – John Victor Read, who you went to visit in the summer,' Lettit went on. 'We knew May very well. She was a KP, just like us. Good young people, all of them, and your grandfather, John, such a nice young man, and so fond of Sarah and Charles – they were his parents – your great-grandparents.'

I had seen those names somewhere, and not just in a photograph album.

'Your great-grandfather, Charles, was something very important in the city.' Cissy picked up the iron with her padded holder. Again her spit skittered across the heated surface. 'He gave it all up so he and Sarah – your great-grandmother – could come here to live. And he was treated so badly, blackballed by his club, having to resign his—'

Lettit stared at her sister in consternation. Cissy sucked in through her teeth, as if she had burnt herself on one of her irons.

'Why?' I asked.

Cissy shot a glance at her sister, before replying dismissively, 'Close-minded, that's what some people are.'

'Well, I think it was very kind of my grandfather to let all these people live in his house,' I said.

'Oh, they were wonderful times.' Lettit turned to her sister. 'Do you remember, Cissy, when Maisie and Young John . . .' She blushed and covered her mouth with her apron.

'What a to-do it was,' her sister agreed.

The two told me how May had come to live with an aunt in Spaxton just when the community was looking for staff. She had been about 14 at the time but had jumped at the chance of a real job in beautiful surroundings, with annual pay of £1, her keep and material for a new dress each year. Her duties included rising at five o'clock every day to light the big range, scrub the kitchen tables and then start the breakfast.

When Belovèd took over the Agapemone from 'Dear Brother Prince' a couple of years later, my grandfather came to live in Spaxton, bringing Charles and Sarah Read and a number of their nine offspring, including 16-year-old John Victor. Over the next few years John finished school, graduated from university and then decided to spend a few months in the Agapemone, working as chauffeur, general factotum and engineer.

'He put in the electric lighting and the mains water,' said Cissy proudly.

He also fell in love with May.

4

A Photograph

Grace Ker left here for Liverpool en route to New York after fortnight's stay.

Entry in the Agapemone diary for
Friday, 22 July 1949

When Toto's niece Grace left for her Long Island home, her American energy went with her. My sisters and I would miss the retired headmistress's praise; she was always admiring our intelligence and the standard of our learning. What I didn't realise at the time was that those fulsome compliments were also subtle criticism of our mother's and uncles' lack of education.

Toto had tears in her eyes as she waved goodbye to the Rolls-Royce as it swept out of the gates just after eight o'clock in the morning, with Uncle David at the wheel and Grace seated beside him. I ran after the old lady as she returned inside and sadly made her way up to what she called her eyrie in the attic.

'Shall I make you tea and toast on your stove, Toto?' I called up after her disappearing feet.

The black-buttoned shoes paused in their climb. 'I'll manage, thank you, Kitty,' she called down. 'But it would be very nice to see you after you've finished your own breakfast.' The shoes continued to plod upwards, like those of a tired mountaineer.

I loved visiting Toto's room, two floors above the dining room. It looked out over the overgrown gardens to the long, stone balustrade that topped the bank, hiding the fruit cages, vegetable gardens and greenhouses. On a clear day, it was possible to see the outline of the Quantock Hills in the distance. We often played a hand or two of rummy or bezique, a complicated card game popular when Toto had been a girl 80 years earlier.

After lunch, I spent 'quiet time' in the orchard helping Edward corral the bullocks Uncle Pat had bought at the Bridgwater market two days before. Then I played a round of solitary croquet with the set that was kept in a room in the stables, along with the bucketful of old, featherless shuttlecocks and the mouse-nibbled badminton net, which had fallen apart when I had tried to unroll it. But it wasn't much fun playing on my own and, besides, I was still worried about Toto, so I returned to her room, lugging a heavy *St Nicholas Magazine* album. This bound copy of six months' worth of the once-popular American illustrated magazine 'for young folks' was one of more than a dozen volumes sent to my mother and her brothers by Toto's brother when they were children in the early 1900s.

'Shall we save the book for tonight?' Toto really was sad. Normally nothing would prevent her reading to me, even though it meant she had to hold the book just inches from her nose in order to see the print clearly.

'Tell me about when you were young,' I asked encouragingly.

I loved her reminiscences about life as a young woman in early Victorian times. Wealthy yet plain, but with a highly developed social conscience, the young Phoebe Ker had worked among the very poorest in the London slums, taking succour to barefoot children, beggars and tramps, and all those 'poor people', she said, who were 'so close to complete destitution'.

'Just like in that clever Mr Dickens' stories,' she added, and then sighed. 'Oh, dear. Those poor children. But, thankfully, things are so much better now.'

Working in the slums was how she had heard about my grandfather. One day she had accompanied her father to one of Dear Belovèd's services in a rented room in Clapton. She had soon become a regular. 'I was at the formal opening of your grandfather's splendid Ark of the Covenant,' she told me.

'Ark of the Covenant?' I had learned about the Ark of the Covenant at school. 'Wasn't that where the Ten Commandments were kept?'

'It was,' replied Toto. 'But it was also what Belovèd – and all of us – called his church in London. That was *our* holy of holies.' She sighed and stared into the distance, as if gazing upon it once again. 'We all gave money toward its building. It was so special.'

'What kind of special?'

'It was where . . . it is very beautiful.' Toto's face became suffused with joy – and regret. 'Oh, they were such happy times,' she said with a sigh.

I had a sudden thought. 'Is that a picture of it in my grandfather's study?'

'I expect so, dear,' Toto went on. 'But it's not used any more. Like so much since Dear Belovèd . . .' She sighed and shook her head, as if in disbelief. 'What a terrible time it was. We just never dreamed . . .'

'What?'

She turned toward me, her eyes huge and melancholy behind the bottle lenses of her glasses. 'That he would . . .' her voice sank to a whisper, '. . . pass over.'

How else would they get to heaven? Besides, not a school holiday passed without the death of one of the elderly women I lived with.

'I had to get Lavita away.'

I was confused. 'Why?'

'She and her dear father had been so close.'

I had often been told the story of my mother's stay on Long Island, where she and Toto had stayed with Toto's brother and his family. It was where my mother had learned to swim and canoe. But I never realised the trip had taken place because her father had just died.

'Didn't Granny mind her going away?' I asked.

'It was a very, very difficult time for everyone, but most of all for your grandmother.'

'Mummy wishes she could have stayed in America for ever.'

'And my brother's family would have had dear Lavita to live with them. But it would never have done, Kitty. Lavita belonged here.'

* * *

The next afternoon, when the house was silent but for a few distant, muffled snores, I decided to take a closer look at this church and sneaked into the room that had been my grandfather's study but was now where my grandmother, mother and uncles took their meals. For once, Uncle Pat wasn't in the armchair by the fire, listening to the afternoon's horseracing on the radio and leaping up between races to dash out to the telephone room, where he would shout his bets down the phone to his bookie. He was busy rounding up his bullocks, which had escaped into the vegetable garden. I had gone to help, but he had shouted at me, so I'd decided to leave him and Edward to chase them back to the orchard by themselves. Sometimes Mummy would make a sudden appearance in search of another library book. Once, Uncle David had appeared through the French windows that looked out onto the little garden outside the chapel. I had ducked down behind the sofa and hidden there until I heard him snoring, then had made my escape. And one day Margaret and I both got trapped between the tall Chinese screen and the upright piano. For once, she had made no effort to make me giggle because she would have got into more trouble than me, as she was so much older.

But today I would be safe. Waa was making and mending our school uniforms for the coming year. With three of us to sew for, that would be sure to take all afternoon. On his return from dropping

Grace at the railway station, Uncle David had driven Mummy and my sisters to their riding lessons – mine was the next morning. It would be supper before they were back because Mummy and Uncle David would be sure to call into a pub on the way home.

I tiptoed to where the small, framed black-and-white photograph of the ornate stone church hung by the mantelpiece. How exotic it looked – dark stone with every corner, edge and flying buttress outlined in a different white stone. Even the tall spire and the baby spires each side of the tower were white. I leaned closer, realising something strange. No gravestones, just manicured lawn. Maybe the picture had been taken before anyone was buried there.

And this was ours! I didn't know anyone else who owned a church! Gosh, we must be important – and rich – I thought.

5

The Ark of the Covenant

It was raining, the kind of rain you only get in England – and perhaps Ireland – the day I paid my first visit to my grandfather's Ark of the Covenant during a family visit home. I was no longer a child and hadn't given this strange building a thought for 20 years. In fact, I had avoided thinking about anything connected to my background and my strange childhood home. But now, married with children and living in Canada, the questions had returned.

As Ann and I rounded the turn into Rookwood Road, it was plain this was no ordinary church. The simple rectangular building, with a high-pitched roof, tower and graceful spire, was so embellished with elaborate decoration it proclaimed an excess I found off-putting, an impression endorsed by the four strange, winged creatures in white stone which stood at the corners of the tower, each one trampling human skeletons underfoot. Higher still, at the base of the spire, another set of the same sculptures, this time in green bronze with wings raised as if ready to launch into the overcast sky.

I glanced down at the book of notes Ann had brought with her.

They explained that the winged man represented Matthew and the humanity of Jesus, the winged lion Mark and the gospel written for the Jews, and the winged ox Luke. The fourth sculpture, the eagle, represented John and the divinity of Jesus. And the skeletons beneath their feet? They were treading down death, pain and sorrow, thus symbolising how man can rise from the material to the spiritual.

On the Tube journey north from her flat, where I had come on my own for a couple of days 'sisterhood', Ann had told me about the church's present tenant. The Ancient Catholic Church is a Christian sect formed in the 1930s, which uses spiritualism in its teaching and also holds services for animals.

'I didn't think our grandfather approved of spiritualism,' I had remarked. Ann shrugged and reminded me that it was the then leader of this sect who had conducted our grandmother's funeral in Spaxton. She also pointed out that the building was actually listed as a registered charity. 'A charity? There's not much that's charitable about this place surely,' I replied.

We hadn't grown up isolated in the Agapemone without understanding that my grandfather's Ark of the Covenant had no charitable purpose having been built with the intention of setting believers apart from an unbelieving world.

Besides, weren't charities supposed to be for the public good? Ann pointed out that it wasn't as if the church had ever made a charitable donation of any kind.

It was years later, as I was doing research for this book, that I came across documents dating from the 1960s showing that Olive Morris, the daughter of the architect who designed this strange house of worship, had persuaded the Charity Commission to list the Ark as a registered charity, as a way of wrenching control of the building from my mother and her brothers. Olive had even admitted in a letter that the application was made without the knowledge of my mother and her brothers 'as they would not approve'.

But that was in the past. Olive was long gone and my sister – and the Charity Commission – was now in charge.

I let my eyes travel up past a huge, arched stained-glass window to the tower's upper stage where more strange symbols were carved, this time in two ornately fashioned circles. 'The fiery chariot of Elijah and the flying scroll of Enoch. They were translated to heaven without death and are witnesses to the expected return of Christ,' I continued reading.

We passed through the arched entrance with its carved exhortation: 'Love unto judgment and judgment unto victory.' Before me stretched row upon row of highly polished pews, each end individually carved. Above me reared an arched ceiling worthy of a cathedral. A band of mosaic in red and gold and black and blue ran round the chancel walls. Incorporated in the design was a pelican, believed to feed its young with its own blood – a symbol of Christ giving life by his suffering – and the mythical phoenix, symbolising the resurrection.

The whole place was suffused with the vibrant colours that emanated from the magnificent stained glass flanking the nave. No 'holy' pictures here, but voluptuous art nouveau designs of roses, lilies, vines, corn and poppies – and were those olives? And pomegranates? Behind me, another window sported angels emerging from a window of fire, bearing the text, 'The sun of righteousness shall arise with healing in his wings.'

'For richness and magnificence of colour we believe it has never been, and it is not likely to be, surpassed,' said another article, culled from an 1896 edition of *The Builder*, an influential architectural and building periodical of the time.

Violet Morris had once told me how the rich depth to the colour in the glass was achieved largely without painting but by layering 'coloured early-English glass'. Margaret had explained that the glass had been designed by the painter and illustrator Walter Crane, who was also a founding member of the Arts and Crafts movement, along with William Morris. Nothing could have prepared me for their actual beauty and impact, however.

'There wasn't originally an altar.' Ann pointed to the rich scarlet cloth draped over a table on the chancel dais at the top of three shallow and delicately curving marble steps. 'There was just a throne.' Her smile was wry.

'Makes sense!' I grinned.

I glanced at the organ. There was something very familiar about it. 'It's just like . . .'

'Eden's?' Ann finished my sentence. 'This one is a Willis organ, too.' Two organs built by the firm whose name is synonymous with England's magnificent cathedrals!

'Our grandfather didn't do things by half, did he?'

We descended the winding steps to a basement suite of offices and spacious meeting rooms. Even here the once gas-lit fittings were ornate and charming. Stained-glass windows in pastel patterns obscured the view from outside.

It had stopped raining by the time we emerged and closed the tall, ornate wrought-iron gates behind us. I glanced back at them as we started up the deserted street and imagined the pushing and the shoving from the sceptical crowds who gathered there following that fateful September day in 1902. I could almost hear the staccato of hooves as my grandfather's coachman wheeled his horses – and my grandfather – away from danger. I thought of the newspaper clippings we had read and chuckled at the words quoting my grandfather's coachman, Alfred Edward Rawlings, all those years ago: 'You're asking for trouble if you go around saying things like that.'

6

❦

Katie's Room

Alice Mary Bacon died, aged 93 years, 11½ months.

Entry in the Agapemone diary for

Friday, 30 December 1949

I missed Alice. Sailing the paper boats she had taught me to make just wouldn't be the same. And I wished I had known when she was alive that Alice had taught herself French so well she could 'speak it like a native', despite never having been to France.

'We were always being complimented on our French,' said Mummy after the old lady had been laid to rest in the churchyard of St Margaret's, Spaxton's village church, two days into the new year. Mummy and I had gone for a short walk along the narrow lanes, with their high, bare hedges, which surrounded the community. 'And it was Alice who taught us.'

My New Year's resolution had been to emulate Alice and surprise everyone at school with my sudden skill. I imagined the look of surprise on my French teacher's face as I prattled away during the first lesson of the post-Christmas term.

'Didn't you learn French at school?' I asked my mother.

'None of us went to school.'

I stopped mid-stride. I frowned and turned to my mother. 'You didn't go to school? Ever?'

Imagine never having to experience those scratchy new clothes that made me feel abandoned at the start of each new term. And at the end of each holiday never again being obsessed with 'This time next month (or week or tomorrow) I will be back at school.'

'We were educated at home.' My mother reached to pull me from the middle of the road. 'How I longed to go to boarding school, Kit. Have school friends, get away, see life. I was determined you three would have what I had longed for as a child.' A sad little smile twitched at her lips. 'You know, I read every Angela Brazil book I could get hold of.'

I had read these tales of 'jolly-hockey-stick' girls at boarding schools after coming across a whole bookshelf of them in one of the attic rooms. Many of them had been inscribed with: 'Lavita, with love from Toto.' They were good stories, although none of the ones I had read seemed to deal with the overwhelming need to cry that I experienced at the start of each new term.

'But why didn't you go to school?'

'We weren't allowed to.' She pursed her lips against indiscretion.

'But why?'

'You'll understand when you're older.'

The same old answer. But just when would I be old enough?

I asked Toto. She explained that Alice had learnt French in order to teach Belovèd's children and that other members of the community had volunteered their services to teach his children English, mathematics, including algebra and geometry, Latin and astronomy (perhaps because Halley's Comet had swung by within hours of my mother's birth). Then there were the obligatory singing and dancing.

'But why weren't Mummy and the two uncles allowed to go to school?' I persevered.

Toto stared at me from behind her bottle-end glasses. 'Dear me, that wouldn't have done at all.'

'Why not?'

'They weren't like other children, Kitty, dear. After all, they were the—' She hesitated and then finished. 'Belovèd's children.'

'Like the princesses, being the King's children?'

Relief flooded her face. 'Yes, my child, rather like the princesses.' I went to bed that night proud of our exclusivity.

Alice's earthly possessions still lay untouched in her third-floor bedroom when my sisters and I returned home for Easter. Margaret and I could resist the temptation no longer. Waiting until the house was silent and the old ladies resting in their rooms, we crept into Alice's bedroom, silently closing the door behind us.

For the next two hours, we rifled through the room: drawers still stuffed with underwear and nightdresses edged with broderie anglaise; the small wardrobe with its meagre collection of shapeless dresses. In her bedside table we found a Bible, a thick caramel-coloured book with no title on the spine, and a whole pile of the squares of brightly coloured paper that Alice had used to fashion the boats.

'Put them down,' Margaret whispered when she saw me fingering the pieces of paper. I was wishing I had paid more attention to Alice's instructions. My sister sighed and tucked the papers into her pocket. 'I'll show you how to make them – but later.'

For the next hour, we forced our feet into the shabby, buttoned shoes lined up tidily under the bed, fastening them with a button-hook we found in the cheap china tray on the chest of drawers. We used the glove stretcher, also in the tray, to prise open the fingers of a pair of tiny elbow-length gloves we came across in the tallboy. We each dangled long strands of black beads around our necks and fought over Alice's only hat, a wide-brimmed black straw affair. We strutted and giggled and collapsed in muffled hoops of helpless laughter before settling down on the floor to play a hand or two of cribbage on the board we had found tucked away in a bottom drawer.

Suddenly, Margaret held up a warning finger. 'Shh!'

She stood up and walked to the bedroom door, opening it slightly.

Through the crack in the door came the unmistakable sound of kettles being filled in the housemaid's cupboard, far away at the top of the back stairs leading down to the kitchens. Rest time was over. Stealthily, we changed back into our own clothes, returning everything to its approximate place, except for the glove stretchers, beads and the pile of squared paper, which we secreted in our pockets. Margaret stuffed the china tray up her jumper.

I was still excited about our adventure at bedtime. Margaret promised to sneak into my room after Waa had turned out my light. We never shared bedrooms. When you live in a mansion with so many empty rooms, after all, there is no point; we simply changed bedrooms at will each holiday, just for the fun of it. Or rather my sisters did. At eight, I was still thought too young for such freedom of choice – anyway, I was scared of the dark and secretly didn't want to sleep in the attic rooms they chose.

'. . . And they lived happily ever after.' Toto smiled at me over the spine of the book of fairy tales. Her hand reached over to stroke my hair. I faked a noisy yawn. 'You're tired, child,' she whispered. The mattress and her knees creaked as she rose. Her hand went to her mouth, covering an answering yawn. 'And so am I.'

'Goodnight, Toto.' I said.

'Goodnight, my child.' The room went dark. I listened as her footsteps trailed away.

Wide awake, I sat up again and waited. Soon, the door opened and Margaret's dark head peered round. 'Kitty?'

'Yes!'

The door closed behind her, plunging us once again into near-total darkness. She was loaded down with her night-time carafe of water, a candle in a holder plus a box of matches, and the china tray we had removed from Alice's bedroom that afternoon. She set everything down on my bedside table, drew up a chair and then struck a match. The room blazed with flickering light. I hugged my knees. I knew what was coming.

'Bonfires!' I exclaimed. I loved this game.

Tipping out the contents of the matchbox, we beg[...]
tower with the matches – four one way, four the other, with[...]
facing alternate directions.

Fifteen minutes later, we had a tower several inches high. We
would have finished sooner, but we had to stop and blow out the
candle twice when footsteps came and went as the old ladies readied
themselves for bed.

'There!' Margaret pronounced at last.

It was an amazing sight. A tower built of matches. I hardly dared
breathe, in case I blew it over.

Handing me my carafe of water – 'Just in case!' – she struck one of
the few remaining matches and held the flame to those on the bottom
layer of the tower. There was a series of little explosions as the first
four match tips caught fire. The flames licked the next layer. They
caught. Soon, the tower was ablaze.

'Eiee!' I shouted as the tower began to tip toward me. I aimed the
water at the now dying fire. Margaret hurled most of the contents of
her carafe at the smouldering pile of blackened matchsticks. Then she
turned on me. Soon we were hurling water at each other.

'Girls!' Waa was standing in the doorway.

We froze. Margaret edged toward the bedside table in an effort to
hide the remnants of our bonfire. I climbed back into bed, hiding my
soaking nightie.

'Sorry, Waa!' offered Margaret.

'We were only playing,' I added.

Our nanny sniffed the air. 'I can smell matches!'

With one hand, Margaret proffered the candle and the near-
empty box of matches. The other she thrust behind her back,
gesturing to me to get rid of the evidence. Hidden behind her, I
began to sweep the burnt matches into a sock I'd providentially
discovered in my bed.

'Really, you girls!' Taking possession of the candle and matches,

d at Margaret's soaking front. 'You're

ight,' Margaret confessed.

ny shook her head. 'I'll be back in five
s.' She turned to leave. 'You girls will be the

g. I could hear it in her voice.

ks later, both of my sisters went fox-hunting and I
decided ... oting on my own. For once, I decided, there would be
no one to boss me around – or acquire the best finds. I waited until
everyone was resting and the only sounds were the ticking of the
numerous clocks throughout the mansion and the muffled snores
from the bedrooms. My goal was the large, comfortable room above
the centre bay window of the dining room, known as 'Katie's Room'.
'You would have loved her; everyone did,' said Waa, when I had asked
who this mysterious Katie had been. I knew that she had died long
before I was born and that I had been named Catherine in her honour.

When I stealthily entered the room one afternoon, it seemed less
crowded by furniture than most of the old ladies' rooms I had been in
– invited and not. I was fascinated by the black-lacquered chest of
drawers set against one wall, covered with Chinese scenes painted in
what looked like gold, and the plain mahogany tallboy by the door.
And the room had a raised dais in front of the window. Anyone seated
in either of the two armchairs there had an unobstructed view of the
garden.

I started with the tallboy. The top drawer was filled with reels of
thread, thimbles and scissors. The next one contained papers, some
covered with sketches in pencil, pen and ink, and even watercolours,
most of which weren't even as good as Margaret's. I delved further.
Spotting a small photograph album, I pulled it free and squatted on
the Indian rug to leaf through it.

It said 'Views' on the front, written in Gothic script. But the first
photograph wasn't of a view. A group of sixteen women were seated in

two rows before a greenhouse. I felt a jolt of recognition as I looked at the picture. I jumped up and looked out of the window, towards the row of cottages flanking the lower lawn. Even from this distance I could see the change in the colour of the bricks, marking where the greenhouse in the picture had once stood. The women wore clothes not too different from those I saw every day in my home – long sleeves and ankle-length skirts – with hair caught up in a bun. Below the photo a row of names had been painstakingly written in copperplate script.

The name Aggie matched the woman on the far left of the back row. I looked closer at the smiling figure in the photo. It was a much younger version of the elderly cook who shooed me from her kitchens when she was busy. The next seven names meant little to me, except the last: May! There was no mistaking my paternal grandmother's determined chin, which people tell me I have inherited, or the glittering dark eyes I now see in my youngest son. I peered closer, fascinated at coming across such incontrovertible proof of our complicated family relationships. Eventually, I turned my attention to the front row. Esther, who had died earlier that year, was on the left and next to her sat a smiling young woman in a black dress with a cameo brooch at her neck. It was Waa. And seated three seats away was Ellen, whom I knew as a fussy, over-burdened elderly woman – nothing like the svelte, attractive woman in the picture.

I began to turn the album's pages. The first few photos were pictures of my home. How different it looked to its ramshackle present. Those manicured, sweeping lawns and shaded walks. I kept turning and came to more photos of people. The woman wore long dresses with leg-o'-mutton sleeves and wide-brimmed hats, the men striped blazers, breeches and straw hats.

In one photo, a young and apparently naked young man sat on a stony beach with his back to the camera, his dark hair glinting in the sun. 'J.V. Read, Esq.' I looked closer. Surely this must be my grandfather! The rest of the snapshots were of groups of young people

– J.V. Read among them, according to many of the captions – picnicking, cycling, playing tennis on the upper lawn, even painting windows. They looked happy and relaxed. And who wouldn't, with such a lot of company. At the very end there was a picture of three young women, one of whom – Phoebe Ker, without spectacles – was chatting by a tennis net. The other two were Nellie Bush and a smiling Emily Hine.

I laid the album aside and delved deeper in the drawer, pulling at the corner of a sheet of paper. 'My dearest sister,' it read at the top. The address was High Street, Orpington, Kent, and the date – it was hard to make out in the old-fashioned handwriting, but it was perhaps 1910, the year my mother was born. The rest of the letter looked like some kind of strange puzzle. It had been written normally, from left to right, but then, to perhaps use all available space, the paper had been turned sideways and the writing continued across the already filled page.

'Katie, I worry so much about you,' I read aloud slowly. 'I cannot bear to think . . .' The next few lines were an impossible jumble, and then, '. . . no understanding . . . I can safely say . . . to your pure nature . . .' Frustrated, I turned the page. 'You know we would welcome you . . . With all my love, your devoted sister, Helen.'

People really were strange back then, I decided. Fancy signing yourself like that! Wouldn't this Katie know who her sister was? I returned the letter to the drawer and pulled out a dark-red bound sketchbook with endpapers decorated to look like marble. In the centre of the first blank page was an ink drawing of an ivy leaf, and within the leaf were written the words: '*Un petit souvenir d'amitié offert au génie et à l'amité par H. Allen à sa bien aimée amie Elizabeth Maber.*' The rest of the pages were filled with sketches of children, young men and women in elegant regency attire, but only the faces were finished, in delicate watercolours: a young man wearing a regency frilly cravat and knee breeches sits holding paintbrushes and an artist's palette; two little girls in bonnets and long dresses dangle titbits for a begging dog. But especially I loved the sketch of three young children – two curly-haired girls, and a boy wearing a cutaway jacket and long pants – caught at the top of a staircase by a tall young man standing framed in a doorway. They looked guilty. The adult wore an expression of mock sternness, the kind I imagined on my father, had he been around to catch us doing something we shouldn't have been.

I stopped, aware of a snuffling sound behind me. Gay must have heard me. Quickly, I shoved everything but the sketchbook back in the drawer, pushed it shut and tiptoed to the door.

'Go away!' I whispered.

A paw scratched in reply.

I opened the door. 'Bad dog,' I whispered. Hiding the sketchbook under my jumper, I crept out. It took me days of struggle with an old French dictionary to get even the faintest idea of the meaning of the words written in the front of the sketchbook.

7

Spiritual Marriages

Elizabeth Maber was born into a wealthy family in Wales in 1801. Her family had embraced the charismatic young Reverend Prince in 1845, when he and his Lampeter Brethren, plus the ever-loyal Reverend Starky, packed the halls and churches of Swansea with their hellfire and brimstone Christianity. Elizabeth, along with her younger sisters Frances and Mary and brother Arthur, was captivated by Prince's vision of an earthly Abode of Love, where the chosen would live out their days safe from the predicted apocalypse – and where she could indulge her love of sketching and perhaps no longer face a drab future as a spinster, dependent on family charity.

Soon Elizabeth had convinced her parents and siblings that their future lay with the handsome young Reverend Prince. Arrangements were speedily made, whereby they would donate their worldly wealth to the brave experiment being attempted in Spaxton, Somerset.

Prince believed he was inspired by the Holy Ghost and that, as its messenger, he was sent to warn of the doom approaching the world.

It was heady stuff to impressionable women like the Maber sisters. Through sheer personality and oratory, he persuaded his increasing numbers of followers to believe that because man was not only sinful but also weak, God had to punish him from time to time with a judgment; hence the floods and plagues contained in the Old Testament.

But, he explained, God was also merciful and always warned humanity of what was to come by sending a messenger in human form. These dispensations had been Adam (the first dispensation), Noah (the second), Abraham (the third) and Christ (the fourth).

He, Henry James Prince, was the embodiment of a fifth dispensation. God had told him that the day of judgment was approaching when Christ would return, this time as the Son of Man as well as the Son of God. But, only those willing to set themselves apart from the world would be saved.

Prince had also captivated the five unmarried daughters of retired wool merchant Josias Nottridge while unsuccessfully attempting to get a permanent Church of England living in Suffolk in East Anglia. His excess of orthodoxy had so concerned the local bishop that Prince had been told he wasn't welcome. Perhaps his rejection fuelled the Nottridge girls' faith, as a year after their father's death, Louisa, 43, Harriet, 41, Cornelia, 36, Clara, 34 – the same age as Prince – and Agnes, 28, took to the road, following wherever Prince and his band of loyal young disciples led.

In their bonnets and furbelows, these five groupies trailed after Prince and his 'brethren' from their home in Suffolk to Weymouth and Brighton on the south coast, and from Swansea in Wales to Spaxton in Somerset, travelling unchaperoned in hired carriages, staying in hotels and lodging houses – often paying Prince's bills as well as their own – and appearing as members of the inner circle surrounding the man whose arrival was heralded by advertisements proclaiming:

'The Lord is at hand'

'The Servant of the Lord will declare the Testimony of Jesus'

'Behold! He Cometh'

What an adventure for these rich, sheltered women! What a defiant gesture!

On 9 June 1845, the cavalcade arrived in Taunton. The sisters put up in the Giles Hotel while Prince and his group stayed at the nearby Castle Hotel. The following morning, Harriet and her sisters had barely finished breakfast when a servant arrived, requesting the 41-year-old spinster's presence before Prince and Starky.

'God is about to confer upon you a special blessing which the spirit has directed us to make known to you,' began Prince on her arrival. 'Before I do that, you must make a solemn promise you will do what is required of you.'

Intrigued, Harriet eagerly agreed.

'You are commanded to marry Reverend Price,' said Prince, explaining that this marriage to one of his most devout followers would be 'in spirit' only and that there would be no carnal relations.

Perhaps, to certain of Prince's sheltered female followers, a marriage 'in spirit' might have seemed the answer to a maiden's prayer. It wasn't a new idea but one based on a passage from St Luke 20:35 in which Jesus says: 'But they which shall be accounted worthy to obtain that world, and the resurrection from the dead, neither marry, nor are given in marriage.'

Prince wasn't alone in advocating unusual marital relationships. Across the Atlantic Ocean, Christian sects with strange sexual observances were also flourishing. They included the Shakers, who practised celibacy, with men and women living together as brothers and sisters; the Oneida Community, which believed in free love; and the Mormons, who practised polygamy. At the core of Prince's teaching was his belief that Christ was about to return to earth and pass judgment on fallible man. He preached fiercely that this imminent arrival of the Second Coming (millenarianism) called for the setting up on earth of a place where the righteous might await the glorious event.

The next sister to be summoned was Agnes, the youngest. She reluctantly agreed to marry another of the brethren, George Thomas, who was just three years her junior. Two days later, their sister Clara was persuaded to marry 29-year-old William Cobbe, who was at that time overseeing the building of the Abode of Love in Spaxton.

The three surprised brides-to-be pleaded to visit their widowed mother in Suffolk before their nuptials. Prince was having none of it. If their mother or brothers dissuaded them, their fortunes would be lost to the cause. Instead, Mrs Nottridge and one of her sons journeyed to Swansea, where they were unsuccessful in dissuading the three from such a mad enterprise.

On 9 July, the sisters married and their individual fortunes of £6,000 each passed into the hands of their husbands, thus effectively under Prince's control. The remaining two unmarried sisters returned to their Suffolk home.

Word of the triple wedding spread. Now, as well as the charismatic Reverend Prince, the curious had three heiresses to gawp at. Once again, the crowds began to swell. But many potential middle-class followers must also have stayed away, rattled by the discontent that continued to sweep the land as a result of the sweeping changes caused by the continued industrialisation of England. And just across the Bristol Channel in rural Wales, memories of the Rebecca Riots a few years earlier were still fresh. Gangs of attackers wearing women's clothing had smashed tollgates in protest against the increasing tolls on turnpike roads. There was enough hellfire and damnation around already without worrying about the afterlife.

So, Prince upped the ante. In Weymouth he roared that only a few were to be chosen and the rest would 'perish in penal fires'. The polite coastal town erupted as those who had been rejected by Prince railed against his arbitrary selection of the 'chosen'. Even the Home

Secretary was asked to intervene. Eventually, tiring of the constant battle with the sinners he had discarded, Prince and the few dozen of his well-heeled followers set off for Spaxton to join more faithful gathering there, including the Maber family.

The community hadn't been in Spaxton long before it became obvious that Harriet and Agnes were pregnant. Prince was furious they had been defiant of his command that the marriages must not be consummated. Did they not appreciate that marital relations were forbidden, he railed; that they were nothing more than fornication? The pregnancies were proof of their disobedience. Only Clara was to escape retribution, either because she and her husband could not have children or they had remained chaste. Agnes and Harriet had to go. Even their husbands, still firmly under Prince's spell, agreed. Agnes fought back.

'If ever you dare to attempt to influence your husband again in acting contrary to my commands,' roared Prince, 'God will crush you out of the way.'

Agnes returned to Suffolk, where she gave birth to a son. Her estranged husband threatened to take the child, but her family swiftly made the boy a ward of court, giving Agnes sole custody. Her unhappy experience wasn't enough to deter her sister Louisa, who, Agnes found out to her horror, also longed to join the Abode of Love. She tried to dissuade her, but failed. Harriet's child died in infancy and, some years later, her young husband was to leave the Agapemone in disgust.

The impressive mansion and attendant buildings weren't ready by the time Louisa arrived in Spaxton. Most of the faithful were housed temporarily in a farm recently purchased by Prince, by now flush with funds thanks to his followers. Since leaving home, she had been bombarded with letters from her family, entreating her to return to Suffolk. Perhaps for this reason – after all, £6,000 was at stake – Prince invited her to stay with him and his wife Julia, where he could keep an eye on her, until the mansion was ready.

* * *

Prince wasn't home on the evening of 10 November 1846. His wife and Louisa had just said goodnight and gone to their rooms when someone entered the house. Louisa assumed it was Prince and took no notice. The next minute, her bedroom door burst open. One of her brothers stood there, accompanied by her brother-in-law and a police officer. She was to come with them, they urged. Her mother was deathly ill. If she dallied, it might be too late.

When Louisa refused to believe them, or go with them, the three men seized her and carried her out. As her unheeded screams rang out over the huge, dark estate, they dragged her, without a bonnet or shawl and wearing only her carpet slippers, to a waiting carriage in which she cowered in a corner despairing. The carriage sped away, the horses galloping through the dark winter night until they pulled up at Moorcroft House, a private sanatorium in Middlesex, where Louisa was admitted, supposedly suffering from delusions.

It took her more than a year to escape. She was swiftly recaptured but not before making contact with the faithful William Cobbe, who persuaded the Commissioners of Lunacy to investigate her case. They found that she was suffering from religious delusion, but her detention was resulting in physical deterioration. The commissioners ordered her release.

Louisa happily returned to the Agapemone and immediately transferred her £6,000 worth of stocks to Prince. She then won a civil suit alleging false imprisonment by her brother. The judge ruled that deviant religious beliefs were not grounds for committal to an asylum.

Her family was to have the last laugh, though: after her death in 1858, the Nottridges successfully sued Prince for the return of her fortune.

8

Katie's Corner

David left for Australia on board the *Derrycunihy*.
Third officer.

Entry in the Agapemone diary for
Sunday, 19 February 1950

We turned away from waving goodbye to Uncle David. I was
bored. I was home alone – my weekend home from boarding
school hadn't coincided with my sisters' visit. And it was too cold for
croquet. Beside me, Mummy surreptitiously wiped away a tear of
loneliness and then told me I had been invited to take tea with my
grandmother. I decided that if I went early, I could perhaps sneak
unnoticed into Granny's boudoir and explore her corner cabinet. If I
was lucky, I could 'borrow' a couple of pieces to show my school
friends.

But that still left me with several hours to kill. I wandered up
through the estate to the vegetable gardens where Edward was
picking Brussels sprouts for lunch from the muddy winter wasteland
that in summer would burst with produce.

'How long have you worked for our family, Edward?'

'Man and boy,' he replied as he carefully cleaned his pocket knife on
the rag he always carried.

'How long's that?'

'More'n 20 years, I reckon. I were barely 14 when I started.' He watched me place the last of the sprouts in the colander he had picked up from outside the door to the kitchens. 'And my father worked here afore me.' Carefully folding the blade into its bone handle, he slipped it into his pocket.

'Did you know Katie?' Lately, I had become intrigued by the letter I had tried to read. Yet I hadn't yet dared return to my solitary rooting in Katie's Room since being interrupted by Gay.

'I did.' He picked up the colander.

Sometimes getting Edward to tell me anything was like getting blood from a stone, even though I thought of him as a friend and companion, one who was always available whenever I felt lonely, or bored.

'What was she like?'

'She were a real lady,' Edward replied.

'Who was she?'

'She was one of the ladies here,' he said. 'But I haven't got time to stand here chatting.'

I fell into step beside him. Soon we had deposited the sprouts on the doorstep, signalled to whoever was in the scullery that they were there and returned to Edward's ever-lengthening list of jobs. I liked helping him wage his ultimately losing battle against the weeds that threatened to overrun the estate's acres of lawn, flowerbeds, greenhouses and vegetable gardens. From him, I learned how to mow a lawn in a pattern worthy of the Wimbledon centre court; how to trench dig; when to prick out seedlings; and how never to lay tools down on the ground, especially not rakes. I had learned that lesson early, when a rake handle had reared up and smacked me smartly on the nose after I had accidentally trodden on its prongs.

But today I didn't fancy helping clean the tidy row of tools kept in the shed at the end of the upper-garden greenhouse. 'I'll have to go, Edward,' I said, as the midday bell rang out over the countryside, signalling to the KP that it was time to assemble for lunch in their gloomy parlour off the kitchens. When I reached the dining room, Gay had completely blocked the entrance by lying full stretch across the doorway. 'I'm bored, Gay,' I told her. She arched her back in reply and lifted a paw in mute appeal. 'Oh, all right.' I bent and scratched the big dog's tummy. She sighed and relaxed back into a deep sleep. Stepping over her, I entered the long, empty room. My grandfather's sorrowful eyes stared into mine from his portrait above the sideboard.

'Stop staring,' I whispered at the picture and ran round the other side of the table and ducked. I crept to the far end and peeked over the top. His downcast gaze met mine again. I ducked and crept to the other end of the long linen-covered table. I popped up. He'd seen me again.

After lunch, I plucked up my courage and decided to return to Katie's Room. When the big house fell quiet, I crept up to the large, central bedroom and quietly opened the door. It took me seconds to find the letter, but I still couldn't decipher it, except to understand that this Helen, who was Katie's sister, obviously wanted Katie to leave here for some reason.

I didn't quite dare remove it; after all, this was someone's letter. No one in the community would ever read anyone else's correspondence, unless, of course, they were invited, like Toto asking me to read aloud her niece Grace's letters from America. The rule was the same at boarding school. Reading another person's letter without permission was an invasion of what little privacy we had. That never stopped me, though (at home, never at school), but at least I did so with a guilty conscience.

Anxious for Gay not to track me down again and make a noise, I slipped out of the bedroom and tiptoed down to the front door, just as Gay rose from her snooze in the sun.

I whistled for her to follow me, and took the narrow, dark path that ran between the high stone wall and the aromatic bay hedge. Soon we were rounding the corner by the East Gate. Ahead lay my destination: Katie's Corner, the little paved garden where she loved to paint.

Katie's Corner was the one place on the estate where the wall was built into the slope of the ground, giving it a uniquely unobstructed view of the outside world: the fields of Holmes farm and, rising behind, the distant outline of the start of the famous Quantock Hills. Only the previous term we had been taught how poets William Wordsworth and Samuel Taylor Coleridge had walked the famous Quantocks.

'Who's there?' Edward looked up from his sweeping, as I pushed my way through the hedge. A pile of mildewed leaves sat in the centre of the little garden, right by what I was looking for. 'Goodness, Kitty, you gave me quite a start appearing all sudden like from the bushes. I thought you were a ghost.' Gay wandered in through the rose arch at the garden's formal entrance. She disliked pushing her way through bushes, as the branches irritated her thin aristocratic skin. 'Oh, my Lord!' Edward pretended to jump at her sudden appearance. 'There's another of you creeping about.'

'Don't be silly, Edward. Dogs can't creep.'

There, just in front of the sundial, was a flat, rectangular stone set in the crazy paving. Carved on it were the words: Sarah, March 1909. Beside it was a second stone, reading: Charles, February 1910. 'These are the names of my great-grandparents, Edward.'

'They are indeed, Kitty.'

'Did you know them?'

'Afore my time, but, by all accounts, they were good people.'

'Are they buried here?'

'Yes, Kitty, they are.'

'Where's Katie buried?'

Edward removed his flat cap and scratched his head. 'I don't rightly know but most likely in the village churchyard.'

'Is this a kind of churchyard then?'

'You could call it that. The old people call it the plantins.'

'The plantings?'

Edward picked up the two boards he always used to carry piles of weeds and scooped the lot into his barrow. 'Yep, the plantins. Ready to rise again.'

'Don't be silly, Edward.'

* * *

So, who was this Katie and why were her family so concerned? The letter I had started to decipher was just one of dozens tucked away in her drawer – how I wish I had read them all. As it is, I must rely on the bones of biographical detail culled over the years long after the letters vanished.

Katie, as she was called from infancy, was born in 1851 and baptised Catherine. She grew up in a loving home in Woodford, Essex. Her father, Henry Bion Reynolds, was a banker's clerk. Her childhood must surely have been a happy one, given her sunny personality. Certainly, she was loved, with brothers and sisters who remained devoted to her.

She loved to read and, like many young ladies of her generation, had been taught the ladylike skills of sketching and painting, hobbies she would enjoy for the rest of her life. She proved a dutiful daughter, staying at home to nurse her mother through her last illness and then caring for her widowed father. She was also naturally devout and never missed church. When she could be spared by her father, she liked nothing better than going to stay with Alfred, her clergyman brother, and his growing family in his large, draughty vicarage in Kingsley, Cheshire.

Katie was in her mid-30s when she first heard my grandfather preach. It was early 1886 and she was visiting Alfred, who had also invited his charismatic clergyman friend to stay and preach the sermon at Sunday matins. Like so many other women had done before her – and would continue to do – Katie found herself caught up in the Reverend Smyth-Pigott's apocalyptic vision for the future, when only the righteous would be saved.

But more than that, she fell deeply in love with the fascinating young clergyman who, it must have seemed astonishing to her, appeared to return her affection (she was by now 35 and judged to be firmly on the shelf).

'She was a sweetheart,' Uncle David would say, and go on to tell me how, during his teenage years, Katie would take him on wonderful holidays to France, Austria and Italy. 'We were very close.'

'I loved her – I think more than my own mother,' my mother once confessed.

Even my grandmother had nothing but praise for her. 'Katie was a good woman. She was such a comfort after your grandfather was gone.'

The old ladies tried to live by the mantras they drummed into our heads – 'If you don't have a good word to say about somebody, say nothing at all' and 'Least said, soonest mended' – but even they, who were known occasionally to express their disapproval of one another, had nothing but good to say about Katie.

'She was such a dear,' Toto would sigh. 'Sometimes I would go and visit her in her studio and sit for hours just watching her sketch.'

It wasn't until recently that I realised that the oil painting I had seen in my childhood home of a church spire in a bucolic country scene was of my grandfather's Ark of the Covenant, painted by Katie. It now hangs in Ann's home.

9

Money Problems

Mary Howlett passed away, aged 82.

Entry in the Agapemone diary for
Thursday, 18 January 1951

The green baize door leading from the upper landing clanged on its hinge as it swung behind me. I winced. My grandmother was blind, but her hearing was legendary. Thoughts of all those tiny treasures drove me on and I tiptoed up the dark, narrow stairs leading to yet another baize door, this time in dark brown. I crossed the corridor outside her boudoir and slowly inched open the door. I hadn't much time, as I was due back at school for the start of term later that day.

My grandmother was seated in her chair by the fireplace, a rug covering her knees. Her false teeth grinned at me from the small saucer set on the table next to the radio. I dropped to my knees and began a slow crawl across the carpet towards the cabinet. I reached for its glass door.

'Who's there?'

I froze.

'Somebody's in here,' said my grandmother. She thumped her walking stick on the carpet.

'It's only me, Granny.' I couldn't stop my voice quivering. 'You invited me to tea, remember?'

I realised she had forgotten, in the fuss of Mary Howlett's passing. I wondered if I should still have come but a summons by my grandmother wasn't something any of us could ignore. Every now and again Uncle Pat's daughter, Angela, who was three years younger than me, and later, her younger sister Victoria, would also be summoned to take tea with their grandmother. But perhaps, I wondered, I should have thought twice about choosing this afternoon to try and get into her corner cabinet.

'It's not teatime yet,' the old lady pointed out.

Twenty minutes to four o'clock. 'I came early in case you had lost your teeth,' I said with sudden inspiration, 'and you needed me to help you find them.'

'Hmmm.' Her hand felt its way towards the saucer holding her teeth. 'I've told you before, Kitty, you will see my treasures when you're old enough and not a day before.'

Sometimes silence is the only answer.

But my grandmother welcomed my company that day – once she had reprimanded me for trying to get the better of her. She seemed to find comfort in telling stories about her life before she met my grandfather, when she was young and death wasn't something she thought about much. Her reminiscences more than made up for failing once again to reach her cabinet, they were told with such relish.

She had been born on Guy Fawkes Day, the 5th of November. I liked the sound of her home in the small village of Sellack in Herefordshire, where her mother was a country midwife. My grandmother let it be known that her father had been a 'gentleman farmer', a myth that survived until recently, when I obtained a copy of her birth certificate. Her father had been an illiterate farm labourer who had signed her birth certificate with an X.

'I was a good scholar,' she said firmly, turning her head in my direction.

'I am too,' I replied, a little defensively.

'And I was good-looking as well,' she went on. She had reddish-brown hair which, even in her 80s, had retained its colour and fine texture thanks, she insisted, to never washing it in anything but rainwater. 'Your grandfather had a third tap installed in the bathroom,' she said proudly. This tap was connected to a barrel outside.

As she rattled on, I sat at her feet imagining this 'young Annie', so bright that after leaving school, she got a job as lady's maid on a local squire's estate.

'Most started off as scullery maids.'

Like my Granny May, I thought.

'I was too clever for that,' she added with such relish even my nine-year-old self got the message. But, she went on, within a couple of years she had grown bored of running around after a grown woman and jumped at the chance to travel as governess to a local family heading to Brazil.

'You liked Brazil, didn't you, Granny?' I prompted, as we tucked into our tea and Madeira cake, which Ellen carried in on a huge tray.

These were the stories I loved best. How she had had to learn to shoot, and once wounded a fleeing attacker who had tried to break into her bedroom through the window. How she had set about two men with her umbrella when they tried to rob her as she was walking across a bridge. 'They soon fled,' she said with satisfaction.

But by the time she returned to England in the late 1890s, she had decided she was capable of more than being a governess and had trained as a nurse at St Peter's Hospital 'for stone and other urinary diseases' in London.

'That's you,' I said, pointing to the framed photograph above the sideboard. She was pictured in her uniform of long-sleeved dress with starched cap and cuffs, and a big bow under her chin.

'Was that before you married my grandfather?' I asked.

But Granny had finished reminiscing. 'That's quite enough for today. Ring the bell for Ellen to clear.'

* * *

A few weeks later I was home once again without my sisters. I had gone to say good morning to my mother and Uncle David.

'We're busy, Kitty,' my mother said in answer to my knock on the drawing-room door before muttering, '*Pas devant l'enfant*' to my uncle. Did they really think I didn't know what that meant?

I set off to hunt for Edward. As I let myself out of the front door, I glimpsed Ellen hurrying to a side door in the tall stone walls holding aloft a huge black umbrella. Few outsiders ventured through the studded doors and the balding, briefcase-carrying figure she let in wasn't the doctor come to see one of the old ladies. I wondered if he was a lawyer, visiting my mother about her divorce. I had overheard her complaining to Waa that our father wasn't giving her nearly enough money with which to raise three children. I followed and watched as Ellen ushered the stranger in through the French windows of my grandmother's dining room rather than taking him to the front door. I reasoned she would only have taken him through the French windows if he had an appointment with my grandmother. I decided to continue my surveillance from her favourite blue cedar overlooking the entrance. The tree would also give me protection from the rain, which by then was falling steadily.

I had barely climbed the tree's lower branches when I caught a glimpse of the stranger behind Grandmother's net curtains, which screened the bay window of her boudoir. It was an hour or more before the man reappeared, this time accompanied by my mother, who looked grave, and Uncle David, who looked angrier than I had ever seen him.

As Uncle David closed the door behind the stranger, he turned and caught sight of me on my perch. 'Get down from there, Kitty,' he commanded.

'I was only playing,' I replied in injured tones.

'Well, go and play somewhere else.'

After lunch, Waa informed me I had been invited to take tea with my grandmother and so, at precisely five minutes to four this time, I obediently knocked on my grandmother's door. 'Have you washed your hands, child?' she asked.

'Yes, Granny.'

'Then please take the chaise.'

The chaise stood beneath my great-grandmother's picture, a winsome charcoal drawing of my grandfather's mother who, legend has it, had been one of the three beautiful Miss Nairnes noted by Queen Victoria in her diary: 'Today I met the three beautiful Miss Nairnes.'

Curiously, my grandmother waited in silence for her tea to arrive. I occupied myself by arranging the small, round three-legged table in front of where I was to sit. The top of the table was covered with an elaborate pattern of fruit and leaves, carved by Olive Morris. I loved tracing my fingers over the wood but didn't like to rest my cup and saucer on it. The carving was so deep it usually ended up slopping my tea into the saucer.

The clock struck four and Granny thumped her stick on the floor. 'Where is everyone?'

'It is only just four, Granny.' I crossed to the tasselled bell-pull and gave it a yank.

'Pull hard,' Granny commanded. 'Ellen is getting very deaf.'

First to arrive was Uncle David, who didn't look pleased when he saw me sitting with my grandmother. When my mother appeared a few minutes later, she didn't seem happy either. I stared back at her, aware, for the first time, how dowdy she looked. She had put on weight, her clothes looked cheap and ill-fitting, and her black hair was badly permed and too short. Worst of all, her generous lips rarely curved in laughter – how different from the faces of the young people captured in those photographs in Katie's bedroom. And on the rare occasions she did smile, splashes of deep-red lipstick stained her still-white and astonishingly even teeth. I found it deeply embarrassing. I thought of photos my mother had shown me of her as a slim, raven-haired young woman in her teens. How could someone change so much? It would be more difficult to recognise her from the photos than Waa, Aggie or Ellen as young women. I watched her as she crossed the room. Her shoulders were hunched as if she were carrying a heavy load.

'What are you doing here, Kitty?' she asked, seeing me watching her.

'I invited her,' my grandmother said shortly.

My uncle and mother exchanged glances.

'But you knew, Mama, we needed to talk to you privately,' protested my mother.

'I know no such thing,' my grandmother retorted.

'Mama!' insisted Uncle David, with a glance in my direction. 'You talked with—' He paused, glanced at me, then seemed to change his mind about what he was going to say. Then continued, '—only this morning. You can't just ignore what has happened.'

What had happened, I wondered. And who had my grandmother talked with? The stranger, perhaps?

'Careful, David,' said my mother, shooting a warning look in my direction.

'Stay where you are, Kitty,' my grandmother commanded, although I hadn't moved. She thumped her stick on the floor again.

Tea was a silent affair. Not even the popular post-war radio soap opera *Mrs Dale's Diary* lightened the atmosphere.

It wasn't until the Easter holidays and all three of us were home from boarding school that I learned the stranger had been the local bank manager. Margaret and I had been playing in one of the attic bedrooms at the top of a steep flight of uncarpeted stairs. We had spread our stable complex across the entire floor. It was constructed from shoeboxes and was complete with show-rings, exercise paddocks and all the horse paraphernalia two horse-mad young girls could dream of. Over the years, we had collected dozens of tin horses, grooms, hounds, etc. and would spend many a rainy afternoon holding everything from foxhunts and gymkhanas to three-day events. This particular day it was a showjumping competition and Margaret's horse, a jet-black stallion inevitably called Black Beauty, was jumping last. My horse had already received four faults (my elbow had caught the top bar of a treble jump). As Black Beauty took off at the last jump, the black-painted pencil representing the take-off bar moved for no apparent reason and rolled to the floor.

'Four faults,' I shouted gleefully.

'It doesn't count,' she retorted. 'It was the wind.'

True, the breeze had got up and was scything through the only source of natural light, a skylight in the far corner, but I wasn't about to let such an advantage go by the board. 'It does so count.'

'Does not.'

Our bickering soon erupted into a pushing match, which progressed to the top of the steep stairs. The next thing I knew, I had lost my footing and was tumbling down. When I realised it was me who was groaning, I found I couldn't stop and, even worse, couldn't catch my breath. I was surrounded by gummy old ladies missing their teeth and wrapped in the shawls in which they each draped themselves during their afternoon rest. Waa elbowed her way through the throng, followed closely by Mummy.

Just as I thought I would surely die from lack of air, my lungs filled. The noise stopped. 'It's all right, Kitty,' said Waa, easing herself onto her knees beside me. There was nothing broken, except the peace of the afternoon, and the old ladies began to wander away.

As soon as she discovered I was all right, Mummy rounded on me. 'Really, Kitty, I can't have this disturbance.'

Waa helped me up. 'Come on, Kitty, you'd better lie down for a bit. You'll be a bit shocked.'

I must have fallen asleep on the sofa in my grandmother's downstairs drawing room, as the next thing I remember hearing was Mummy and Uncle David whispering in the passage outside. They were discussing the local bank manager. I soon realised they were probably talking about the man I had seen arriving when I had been home from school previously – it was so unusual for a stranger to be admitted into the community (I knew what the doctor and the undertaker looked like, so could tell it wasn't either of them) that it wasn't hard to put two and two together. I pricked up my ears.

'Not again!' said Uncle David. 'Mama would have given it to him. After all, she always does!'

'I know, but things are very difficult for Pat at the moment,' replied my mother.

'But knowingly bouncing cheques! That's going too far, Lavita.' Uncle David went on to say how humiliating it was for my grandmother to be obliged to receive a bank manager who had come to complain that one of her sons was bouncing cheques.

'I know, but don't forget he's desperate at the moment. After all, he has a young daughter as well as a new baby,' said Mummy.

'You've got three daughters,' Uncle David pointed out. 'And you don't get nearly the financial handouts our brother does. What's to prevent Pat getting a job? He certainly doesn't have to spend his life gambling, drinking and making life miserable for his unfortunate wife, even if she isn't quite one of us.'

'No, Babe isn't one of us, but don't forget, David, she and Pat have done better than we have when it comes to marriage. At least they're not divorced. Let's just forget it and say nothing.' But Uncle David hadn't finished. It was time, he went on, that their brother realised that even though the community was no longer hounded by journalists it wouldn't take much for them to begin making a nuisance of themselves again.

I heard my mother's sharp intake of breath. 'Imagine what a field day the press would have if this got out.'

I frowned. I couldn't imagine why the press would be interested.

* * *

My oldest sister was not only good at sewing but also had an eye for fashion. Ann was becoming nearly as good as Waa at turning lengths of material found in some neglected drawer during our rooting expeditions into dresses and skirts. Now she was consumed by the task of getting together a wardrobe for her approaching departure to stay with our father.

I wasn't the least bit interested in clothes unless they were jodhpurs, but I envied Margaret's creative talents. She could conjure up a herd of wild horses, manes and tails flowing in the wind, with a few strokes of a pencil. She had constructed working puppets of Queen Victoria and Prince Albert, complete with strings, which stood more than a foot high and were dressed in outfits made from the clothes we had found rooting. Surely she would be able to help me, I had decided, staring at the page in the *Good Housekeeping* magazine Mummy had bought on impulse one day. The competition was for children up to and including age ten, and involved drawing a clock. Margaret agreed to lay out the points of perspective. I made a first attempt at the drawing and then Margaret helped me improve it.

A few weeks later, I found a parcel waiting for me on the hall table. I tore it open and discovered, to my delight, I had been awarded second prize in the magazine's monthly competition, a copy of the *Good Housekeeping Book of Fairy Stories*, which had been newly selected, edited and translated by P.H. Muir, with decorations by Geoffrey Rhoades. The slim volume had been published by Gramol Publications Ltd of London and Cheshire. Noted on the flyleaf, in my best handwriting, is: 'Awarded to Kitty Read for being second in *Good Housekeeping*'s monthly competition.'

Ann was busier than ever with Waa's sewing machine that Easter holiday, turning a shawl she had filched into a dress. She was constantly washing her hair, whether it was dirty or not, and buffing her nails – and was she wearing lipstick when she left to stay with a school friend?

Ann and Margaret often excluded me from their whispered confidences – and their arguments – but that year my isolation seemed worse than ever. They were hardly ever at home; they even spent a couple of weeks in the summer with our absent father's parents, Granny May and Grandpa John. I had begged to be allowed to go too, but my mother had said three was too much for our grandmother and I would have to wait for another time. But when they returned, they seemed even more at odds with themselves, each other and everyone else. Ann spent almost every waking hour at the home of a school friend in the village.

I hated venturing beyond the estate. It took all of my courage to make the fewer than 100 yards to the village shop to spend my meagre pocket money on bottles of Tizer, the vivid-orange fizzy drink, and Crunchie bars. The owners of the shop, a mother and daughter, were never anything but friendly but, oh, how I dreaded running the gauntlet of village children lingering confidently in groups outside the shop. If I spotted them before they saw me, I would turn tail for the security of the community. If I had been seen, I marched past them, nose in the air, ears attuned to the slightest giggle of ridicule.

To add to my misery, Margaret had suddenly become a perplexing whirlwind of confusing emotions: ecstatically happy one moment, furiously angry the next and then tearfully despairing. For several days, she was incapacitated by terrible headaches, which Waa said was 'Just like dear Ruth,' as she hurried to fetch a tablet and apply cold compresses.

Later I overheard Mummy and Waa discussing how difficult girls could become with the arrival of 'the curse', along with other changes

I had learned about during a series of highly embarrassing talks by the school matron.

It wasn't until years later that I learned Ann had found out the truth about our strange home during the previous term and had searched the school encyclopedias to understand the word Agapemone. There she had read the whole story and told Margaret, who had found the revelations upsetting.

10

Johnny Pigott

As a child, I believed what I was told: that my grandfather had been a wonderful man loved by all. It seemed only right since everyone talked about him as Dear Belovèd.

According to my mother, he had been born a gentleman into the Smyth-Pigott clan of north Somerset landed gentry. He was also, she said, connected to some of the kingdom's great aristocratic families. As a result, she was often gently insistent that her own daughters were 'ladies' and should always behave as such. She even relayed to us the injustices her father had suffered as a boy. How her father, John Hugh, the youngest of three boys, had had to attend Rossall School, then a brand-new boarding school in the unfashionable northern seaport of Fleetwood in Lancashire, rather than Eton, where male members of the family had traditionally been educated.

What she didn't tell me was the reason for his apparent banishment, perhaps because she never knew. By the time my grandfather was old enough to be sent to boarding school, family charity was running out. The Smyth-Pigott family had taken in John

Hugh, his mother and older brothers when the boys' father, Henry, had first shown signs of madness, now thought to have been brought on by gonorrhoea. Soon Henry was declared insane and committed to a lunatic asylum, where he died. His youngest son, my grandfather, John Hugh Smyth-Pigott, was just five. It was no wonder England's premier private school was no longer an option.

My grandfather didn't excel at school. He won no academic prizes, failed to represent the school or his 'house' at sport and left aged 18. Within weeks, he had signed on as a seaman aboard a sailing ship. In 1870, calling himself plain Johnny Pigott (he dropped the Smyth part of his hyphenated surname), he set off to see the world. Just as 100 years later legions of young men and women would 'drop out' in search of nirvana, so my grandfather shrugged off his upper-class background and immersed himself in the tough world of the ordinary sailor.

As I grew up and the community dwindled, my mother and I were thrown together and she began to tell me the tales her father had told her, of his seafaring adventures and attempts at gold prospecting. I wish now she had seen the articles he wrote for his divinity college magazine about his travels and read for herself his descriptions of his adventures. But my mother had been dead for years by the time I tracked these down, written in his recognisable handwriting and archived at the University of Nottingham. 'Lost in the Bush', my grandfather's article about his gold prospecting days in Cawarral Goldfield in Central Queensland, Australia, was published in the *St John's Magazine* in December 1880. The huge Cawarral Goldfield, discovered in 1860, stretched from the northern branch of the Fitzroy River to the sea as far north as Yaamba. My grandfather and a friend named Arthur had set off one morning on a twelve-mile hike to a shanty town then known as Cawarral Diggings to buy more rations. He wrote:

> Our attire was selected rather with a view to coolness and ease
> than elegance. It consisted of soft white felt hats, flannel shirts,

moleskins [trousers] and good large Blucher boots; and if I add to these two knives, two pipes, some tobacco and matches, and a one pound note, you have our whole equipment before you . . . Our surroundings continuing to raise our spirits: the deep blue Australia sky, bright sun, green grass, grand trees, cockatoos, white and black, screaming a grand operatic chorus, exquisitely coloured parroquets [*sic*] flying from tree to tree, iguanas lazily sunning their hideous bodies, any amount of flyers and wallabies springing about, and now and then an Oldman Kangaroo leisurely stopping to take a good look at us, then solemnly going about his way as if he had the cares of nations on his old head; whatever we were doing we seemed so friendly and happy together that Arthur and I felt like two Alexander Selkirks, 'monarchs of all we surveyed'.

But the young men got lost:

> . . . finding ourselves in a regular cul-de-sac of thick scrub. We now decided on retracing our steps to the plain in order to take a new departure from it to search for the much longed-for water hole. This plan, simple enough in theory, proved quite a failure in practice. Immediately we turned to go back, the cattle track, which had seemed so simple as we went, began to branch off in every direction.

Just as they began to despair, lost with night closing in and no water, it began to rain. They were saved and after another 36 hours stumbling about lost in the bush, they came across the camp belonging to a couple of men fencing in the area. They were escorted into Cawarral, where they picked up their supplies and returned to their camp.

In this, the second article of his to appear in *St John's Magazine*, published in 1881, my grandfather told of sailing up the West Coast of America aboard the SS *Oregon* as it threaded its way through a maze of buoys. Just a few weeks earlier, the SS *Great Republic*, then the largest sailing ship in the world, had run aground in the same area.

Their ship eventually reached the town of Astoria and my grandfather and a shipmate disembarked. They found that renting a room was costly, at $10 a week.

> . . . we must get work without delay, or we would soon get no dinner. This knotty point being settled we went downstairs and following the sound of a very noisy bell we found ourselves in a large room in which two tables were groaning with luxuries. The menu was something like this – clam soup, salmon, beef, mutton, veal, pork in many forms, plenty of vegetables and the inevitable apple pie. Everybody seemed in a terrible hurry, for we had scarcely finished our soup, when most of the men got up to leave, having, as we calculated, eaten in eight minutes, an enormous dinner of four courses, while we, although making all possible speed, couldn't accomplish it under thirty minutes. However we took heart, as it was our first attempt and hoped that even in this most difficult case the old proverb 'Practice makes perfect' might hold good. We now sallied forth in search of employment and found as the results of our first enquiry that the general opinion was that there were many more men in Astoria than there was work for. We were not in the least disheartened by this as the same story meets you all over the world if you only go to the right quarter, i.e. somewhere contiguous to a liquor bar, – for when the drink curse has taken away a man's self-respect, his energy soon follows and he loves nothing so well as to loaf about within the range of the poisonous odours, so that he may be within hail if some 'good fellow' half-seas-over, should come along and call him a drink.

Johnny Pigott and his friend soon tracked down the kind of area they were looking for: a fishing cannery by the docks. The manager of Booth's Cannery told the two young Englishmen that, yes, there were plenty of men looking for work but that 'the majority of them were most anxious that they should not find any'. The manager then suggested they travel further down the coast on a newly arrived steamer which was picking up returning boats filled with salmon on its way to a nearby seining station. There they met 'Poker' Smith.

'His sobriquet of "Poker" came from his unfortunate predilection for that ruinous game of chance, which is another of the curses of America,' commented my grandfather.

My grandfather was hired immediately on $45 a month and his friend was assured that work would also be found for him. 'We went aboard the steamer and off [back] up to Astoria greatly pleased with the results of our expedition,' he concluded. But by 1879, my grandfather had grown tired of his rough, knockabout life. He had also, he confessed to my mother, 'got religion' while staying in a Seamen's Mission in New York.

Suddenly, this life of adventure seemed aimless for a man just turned 27. And he was losing friends. His fellow sailors couldn't abide 'God-bothered' seamen in the forecastle. He decided to return to England, no doubt to the relief of his widowed mother.

* * *

My grandfather was 28 when he enrolled in the London College of Divinity in 1880. The Islington theological college had been founded fewer than 20 years previously as an evangelical establishment to train mature students for the Anglican priesthood, with the idea that many of them would perhaps become missionaries. That must have appealed to my restless grandfather and he threw himself into his studies, winning several academic prizes and finishing first in his year. His unusually quiet voice added power to his increasingly compelling sermons as well, while his dark, mesmerising eyes set in his long ascetic's face added to his attraction. And as a bachelor with what surely would be a rosy future within the established Church, Seminarian Pigott must have appeared a catch to mothers of unmarried daughters in the locality – and no doubt also to the daughters.

After ordination as deacon in St Paul's Cathedral in December 1882, my grandfather was given a prestigious position at St Jude's in Hackney, a church he already knew well from its involvement with the college. A year later, Deacon Pigott was ordained a priest, again in St Paul's, and appointed curate at St Jude's.

At first, his vicar couldn't speak highly enough of Reverend Pigott. 'He had a pleasant personality and was a born leader,' Reverend Daniel Bell Hankin recalled many years later. 'His ministry was much blessing to many people, over whom he exercised an influence that was almost mesmeric.' He was also enthusiastic and unconventional, even with his evangelical training. He began to lead nights of prayer.

He did not, however, take kindly to criticism. 'He was a strong-willed man, determined to get his own way, and, I may add, generally got it,' Reverend Hankin ruefully acknowledged. But less than two years into his curacy, Reverend Pigott walked away from the established Church. He wasn't alone. Two other enthusiastic and unconventional young clergymen also swapped the pulpit for the street-corner soapbox. The three of them joined the Salvation Army.

In 1865, as regular churchgoers became appalled at the sudden influx of the shabby and unwashed into their place of worship, William Booth, an Anglican clergyman who had abandoned his living for the streets and its shifting population of destitute, hungry and homeless, founded The Christian Mission in east London, later to become the Salvation Army.

By the time Reverend Pigott joined 'the Army', it was becoming almost respectable, to the point that there had been some mention of its amalgamation with the Church. Once again, my grandfather must have seemed a great catch to this upstart organisation. By July 1884, he was leading Holiness meetings twice a week and had converts rolling on the floor in spiritual ecstasy. In September, by then a staff captain, Reverend Pigott took part in an evangelical expedition led by Booth's son Bramwell to Cambridge University, where notice was taken of the young Pigott by one of the undergraduates, a devout young man called Douglas Hamilton. In the December, my grandfather was chosen to accompany 'general' William Booth himself and some of his close associates to a Holiness Convention in Brighton on the south coast. Then he was sent as special envoy to Norwich to raise money to rid the Army of its debts. He rode to the Houses of Parliament bearing a temperance petition signed by thousands of Salvation Army stalwarts. He even preached in Yeovil, Somerset – perhaps his mother, who lived not far away, turned out to hear her devout youngest son preach. He made many moneyed friends within the Salvation Army faithful, among them wealthy company director and stockbroker Charles Stokes Read and his wife, Sarah.

In June 1885, now 'major' Pigott, he was appointed vice-principal of the Salvation Army's training homes in Clapton, north-east London, and was surely destined for even greater heights within the organisation. So why, by September of that year, had my grandfather resigned from his position and written the Army off as a 'rope of sand'? And why did the Salvation Army commissioner complain years later that the young major had proved 'careless, slovenly and unreliable' and had failed to keep up with his correspondence? But, worst of all, the commissioner accused Pigott of causing a young man's death by his insistence on constant prayer and fasting.

Did news of this reach Bramwell Booth, who meted out punishments severe enough to anger my grandfather into resigning? Was he becoming disillusioned with a once radical Army that appeared to be growing ever closer to the religious establishment? Claims that the Army and my grandfather fell out over his spiritualist leanings are surely without foundation. My mother remembered clearly how, as a child, she witnessed her father's fury when he discovered some of his followers surreptitiously trying out an Ouija board. 'I think it's the only time I ever saw him angry,' she told me.

My grandfather's resignation was accompanied by those of several others, including the devout Mr and Mrs Read. What did they think, I wonder, of this young man of God's next move, which was to rejoin the Anglican church?

The former 'major' John Pigott began to network among his former Anglican friends and acquaintances, among them Reverend Alfred Reynolds, who had charge of a living in Kingsley, Cheshire. My grandfather paid Reynolds a visit, one of several that autumn. Alfred invited his friend to preach the Sunday sermon, which was 'much appreciated' by the congregation. Another visit coincided with that of Reynolds' spinster sister Catherine, the eldest girl of five siblings. Was it a set-up?

Catherine, now in her mid-30s, must have already reconciled herself to the life of a spinster. But the handsome young priest appeared attracted to the tall, plain young woman with a wonderful personality. A year older than him, she seemed so steady and empathetic to his beliefs and aspirations. Above all, she was such a good listener. Perhaps, as the weeks went by and he pursued her back to the family home in Woodford, Essex, my grandfather also decided that marriage to the sister of a clergyman might help his own reconciliation with the Church.

On 14 August 1886, Reverend Reynolds officiated at the couple's marriage in the parish church of West Hackney, where my grandfather was living at the time, most likely courtesy of the Reads, who owned or leased extensive property in the area.

The marriage was obviously popular with the bride's family: the handsome young priest was suitably devout and well-born. Catherine's widowed father and her younger sister, Helen, were happy to be witnesses to the ceremony. Having one of three daughters married must have been a relief to the father.

Three months later, Reverend and Mrs Pigott left for his first appointment since his successful reconciliation with the Church of England. After a rough November crossing of the Irish Sea, they arrived in Dublin, where my grandfather was to take up a position as curate at the Anglican mission in Townsend Street, Dublin.

It was a tough job, even for someone so familiar with the vagaries and difficulties of missions. He had, after all, stayed in a number of them during his knockabout years. But my grandfather had moved on and later confessed to my mother how he hated the pitiful pay, endless hours and spartan accommodation. Perhaps he also felt bad for the deprivations to which his wife was being subjected and decided the appointment was a deliberate attempt by a vengeful Church to punish him for turning his back on the Anglican faith.

'He was recommended to me by friends in whom I had the fullest confidence, who wished him to return to the Church of England or Ireland after his lapse to the Salvation Army,' wrote mission priest Reverend Henry Fiske many years later. But Fiske and the charismatic young priest took an instant and palpable dislike to each other. Six weeks later, my grandfather left.

'Mr Pigott left me at my own desire, as he held doctrines, as I found out, which were entirely contrary to my own and which I thought calculated to undermine the faith of my flock,' said Fiske.

Now out of work, my grandfather had no option but to take his wife back to Cheshire and the hospitality of his clergyman brother-in-law. Alfred was delighted to see the couple and asked John Hugh if he would like to once again give the Sunday sermons. But news of Pigott's hasty departure from Dublin had already reached the Bishop of Chester's cloisters. The bishop quickly sent a letter warning Reverend Reynolds against the idea. Alfred had his own career to think of and my grandfather was barred from the Kingsley pulpit.

There was nothing for it. Reverend Pigott returned to Dublin, intending to poach members of his erstwhile superior's flock. But not even that was a success, although, coincidentally, news of the goings-on in the mission reached the ears of Douglas Hamilton, who three years earlier had been so impressed with the then Staff Captain Pigott's performance at the Salvation Army's evangelical expedition to Cambridge University.

Hamilton, now a devout Agapemonite, was visiting Ireland on holiday and came to hear of Pigott's trials at the mission, perhaps from my grandfather himself. Whether Hamilton approached the unhappy clergyman about joining the Agapemonites isn't known. Maybe the Reverend Pigott had picked up a copy of writer and editor Hepworth Dixon's book, *Spiritual Wives*, published in 1868, or even seen a copy of his article, also entitled 'Spiritual Wives', published the same year in *The Athenaeum*, a weekly literary periodical.

Prince, now elderly and infirm, was no longer able to make the journey to London to preach to his followers there. The sect needed a London pastor. Perhaps Hamilton had found one.

The Agapemone

My grandfather John Hugh
Smyth-Pigott (Dear Belovèd)
in his later years

John Hugh Smyth-Pigott as
a young man in his seminarian
uniform in the 1880s

The 'KP', probably taken in the early 1900s: Margaret (Waa) Davis
(seated, second from left), Ellen, my grandmother's personal maid
(seated, fifth from left), my maternal grandmother Elizabeth
(May/Maisie) Link (standing, far right)

John Victor Read, community
chauffeur and odd-job man, and
my paternal grandfather

Phoebe (Toto) Ker, Nellie Bush and
Emily Hine by the tennis net on
the upper lawn in the early 1900s

My grandmother Ruth Annie
Preece in her nurse's uniform
in the 1890s

The 'Holy Family': (from left)
Belovèd with Power on his knee,
Glory seated on the step, Lavita in
Ruth's lap, 1910

My uncles Pat (left) and
David (right)
with my mother
Lavita *circa* 1919

A costume picnic at the Agapemone in June 1912: Charles Stokes Read (standing at rear, second from left), Waa (fourth from left), Eva Paterson (fifth from left), Katie Pigott holding Lavita (centre standing) and Toto (seated on far right). Glory (Uncle David) is astride the donkey and to his left is Power (Uncle Pat)

Children at the 'A', dated 1916: my father, Leopold (Polo) Read (far left), my mother, Lavita Smyth (third from left), Uncle Pat (fifth from left) and Uncle David (far right)

Eden in the 1940s

Grandmother Ruth,
circa 1940

Prior to our move to the Abode of Love, I meet my father, 1945: (from left)
Uncle Stephen (my father's brother), my sister Ann, our Great Dane Gay,
my sister Margaret, my mother, my father, me aged four, and Granny May

Me, aged six, outside Eden's entrance

Waa with Gay, *circa* 1950

Me with Pinto

Left: The Ark of the Covenant,
Rookwood Road, Hackney,
north London

Below: Stained-glass windows at the Ark of the
Covenant designed by Walter Crane, leader of
the Arts and Crafts movement
(© TimGoffe.com)

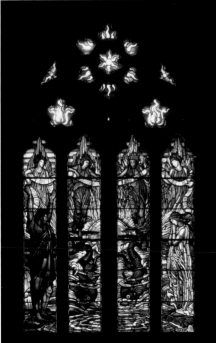

My sister Ann's wedding: me (far left)
and my older sister Margaret (far right)

My mother in 1972

11

Outsiders

King George VI died suddenly at Sandringham.

Entry in the Agapemone diary for
Wednesday, 6 February 1952

I rarely chose to take tea with the fearsome Emily, but Uncle David had driven Toto into town to get her glasses mended, which she had stepped on the night before, and it was Edward's day off. I wouldn't normally have been home from boarding school anyway but for some long-forgotten reason we had been given an extra couple of days' holiday.

'Enter,' commanded the old lady, in answer to my tentative knock.

I poked my head around the door. 'It's me.'

'I can see that.' Emily sat by her fireplace, wrapped in a knitted shawl, her yellow-white hair minus its hair net.

Steam rose from Emily's kettle as it boiled on the little paraffin stove. All the old ladies kept stoves in their rooms, even though the entire mansion was centrally heated. (The rush of water into kettles from the tap in the housemaid's cupboard at the top of the kitchen stairs at precisely ten minutes to four every day was the signal to stop rooting, or climbing over the roof, or whatever other mischief my sisters and I were up to.)

Emily's Royal Doulton tea service was already laid out on the little gateleg table. On a plate lay what I knew from experience would be very stale arrowroot biscuits. It was stiflingly hot. Perhaps I should have postponed my visit until the holidays, but it was too late to back out now.

'Would you like me to take tea with you?' (You never said 'have' tea. That was slang!)

'That would be very nice, Kitty.'

I crossed to the stove and asked whether I should make it.

'If you would be so kind.'

I knew Emily preferred her tea without milk and sugar, but knew better than to assume. 'Will you take milk and sugar?' I also knew better than to say 'Do you want' – a very vulgar modern habit.

With tea served to her satisfaction, Emily took a sip and then muttered, 'Not as good as in your grandfather's day.' She sighed. 'But then nothing is.'

She replaced her cup in its saucer and glared across at me. 'That was tea: 60 per cent black, 30 per cent Lapsang Souchong and 10 per cent green.'

I thought quickly. Which of her 'stories' would be least likely to get her worked up? I was sure I would get blamed if she ended up throwing the china about. 'What was it like being a nurse in Victorian times?' I asked.

Emily related the story she had told me many times before: how she had trained at St Thomas' Hospital in London in the early 1880s. Normally, she loved talking about those days, when she was young, energetic and eager to serve, but today it seemed she wanted to boast about how her nursing skills led her to being asked to nurse John Brown, Queen Victoria's favourite servant.

'I thought he lived in Scotland,' I said. I had heard the story before and still couldn't work out what was so special about a servant who sounded very rude most of the time. (Now, having seen *Mrs. Brown*, the film about the relationship between the Queen and her Highland servant, how I wish I had paid more attention.)

'He was a Scotsman to the core, but he had accompanied the dear Queen to Windsor and caught a bad chill.'

'How did you get invited to take tea with her?' I nudged.

'She wanted to say thank you for nursing Mr Brown.' She pointed to a small framed photograph of 'the dear Queen' hanging beside her bed.

'And she gave you a signed photo of herself,' I finished.

'Hmm,' said the old lady, 'at least you know how to pay attention!'

I reached for yet another of the soft and slightly musty-tasting biscuits.

Emily glared. 'Yes, you may have another, young lady,' she said repressively, but with a surprising twinkle in her faded blue eyes. She indicated the teapot. 'Come on, girl. Where are your manners?'

I swallowed quickly. 'Would you care for another cup, Emily?'

'That would be very nice, dear.'

* * *

The house was quiet. Ethel's pantry was deserted. I crept down the dark passage into the little vestibule outside Eden and paused at the huge clipper on top of the roll-top desk. I spread my arms. It must have been at least four feet long. So, this was the kind of ship my grandfather had sailed on. I pulled one of the looping strings. A sail moved. Half-closing my eyes, I pulled another, and another, gradually setting the sails on a different course, as I imagine my grandfather would have done.

I soon tired of this make-believe and quietly let myself out of the double doors leading into Eden's small walled garden. The sky was blue and the water in the birdbath remained unfrozen, despite the temperature, which hovered just above freezing. I picked a long, waxy leaf from the magnolia tree and began to sail it around the shallow, circular pool of water, conscious of the impatient twittering of songbirds wanting a drink.

I missed Ann, who had left home the previous year. Not because she had ever played with me much, but simply because she was my older sister, whom I admired and looked up to. Margaret was my playmate, despite the five-year age gap, but Ann also represented 'family' in a deeply satisfying way. I am eternally grateful to her for her refusal to ever lose touch with her younger siblings, for being the linchpin of our strange and fractured family.

But it wasn't Ann's absence that troubled me that chilly morning: my mother had taken the bus into Bridgwater the previous morning and had got a job in the town's jam factory. A jam factory! 'All honest work is honourable, Kitty,' she had chided me. 'Anyway, beggars can't be choosers.' None of my school friends' parents worked in factories. Then there was the factory's sickly sweet smell, which would surely cling to her clothes – even though, I had to admit, it would be better than the stink from the cellophane factory, the town's other main employer.

Was such a drastic step necessary? My home had a faded luxury, which at times verged on the scruffy, but surely we were hardly beggars. Leaving the birdbath to the birds, I wandered through the gardens to the stone balustrade, which separated the formal gardens from the fruit cages, greenhouses and vegetable gardens.

My mother only lasted a week, preferring to work in the town's bra factory. When she told me, I wasn't sure which was worse. At ten years old and thin as a rail I had no use for bras, but I would have enjoyed the jam.

My mother and her brothers had been brought up in the lap of luxury, surrounded by those who catered to their every want. Their lifestyles were dependent on my grandfather's followers cheerfully donating all their worldly wealth to his Abode of Love. And by the 1950s, what had been considerable sums 50 years earlier had all but been used up, with the result that my grandmother and her three adult children had very little to draw on to support my grandfather's aging followers. The inevitable monetary shortages were met sometimes by wills of the recently departed but more often by selling off land, property, furniture, even the chapel organ. The funds raised were used first to meet outstanding community bills – many a valuable piece of furniture or silver paid our school fees, as well as for the coke which fed the mansion's huge central-heating boiler. Any cash left over from a sale went towards Uncle Pat's immediate debts first and whatever remained was divided between Uncle David and my mother – and Uncle Pat again. Eventually, the struggle to make ends meet became so difficult that, apart from reminders for our school fees, my mother simply hid any incoming bills in a desk drawer. Out of sight truly became out of mind.

I had no understanding of the cost of running such a huge estate and certainly no concept of inflation, and what that had done to funds donated up to a century earlier. The appetites of my home's aged residents were a shadow of what they must have been back in Victorian days when the ladies were in their youth, but most still ate – and expected to eat – heartily. The huge central-heating boiler needed mountains of coke to be fed into its glowing innards each day to warm the huge mansion, which meant hiring someone to stoke it morning and night.

I hadn't counted on Uncle David as an ally when it came to my mother's jobs. He too disliked his sister working on an assembly line and did his best to come up with alternative sources of income – none too successful until, one day, he tentatively approached his mother with an idea; one so radical for this closed community that it required a seismic shift in thinking. My uncle had heard of a young couple, Hans and Trudel Lederman, who had a young son and were having difficulty finding somewhere to live. Perhaps they could rent one of the cottages bordering the lower lawns, he suggested tentatively. After all, the North Gate, Mary Howlett's former home, had already been sold and separated by a sturdy fence. Suggesting someone live within the community, which had always been closed to outsiders, was quite another matter, however.

The Ledermans, my uncle told his mother, were a Jewish family from Germany still facing discrimination, even though the husband was earning good money repairing agricultural equipment and would be certain to pay his rent on time. He went on to say that many members of the young couple's family had been killed by the Nazis. (I was to learn many years later how Hans and Trudel had made their way to England separately just before war broke out and that Hans had even spent some months in Buchenwald concentration camp prior to escaping to England.)

Granny felt for her saucer and replaced her teacup. She turned in her eldest son's direction. 'You have my permission, David, to offer them one of the cottages,' she said, before murmuring to herself, 'I know only too well what it's like to be "different".'

I thought of my father's mother, a bustling, competent but sharp-tongued woman, and remembered meeting a school friend's apple-cheeked grandmother, who was like something out of a storybook. I gazed at the blind old woman before me, who wore clothes long out of fashion and was never without her veil. Yes, my granny was certainly 'different'.

* * *

For years, I had longed for a playmate my own age. It would be nice to have someone to boss around, even if it was a six-year-old boy. But I wasn't sure I liked the idea of strangers in my private playground.

It was summer when the Ledermans moved in. I was flying through the air on the swing hung from a branch of the cedar on the upper lawn when I saw Mummy picking her way towards me through the tangle of weeds and grass. Walking beside her was a small red-haired woman and a man who looked just like James Mason. Between them walked a small red-haired boy.

'Come and meet Mr and Mrs Lederman and their son, David,' my mother called.

I scraped my sandals through the dirt to slow myself and jumped off the worn wooden plank with what I hoped was amazing athleticism. Wiping my hands on my jodhpurs, I stretched out a hand first to the man and then the woman. 'How do you do?'

'It is very good to meet you, Kitty,' said Mr Lederman in a German accent I recognised from films shown at the local cinema. As he spoke, I caught the glint of a gold tooth. 'This is David,' he said. 'Say hello, David.'

The boy scowled shyly up at me.

'Hello, David.'

'We hope you will come round and see us,' said his wife. 'Perhaps you like to watch television?'

I had longed for a television set. Violet and Olive Morris, ever in the vanguard of any technological advance, had one in their East Gate home and occasionally invited me to sit with them in total darkness and watch the flickering screen. But it just wasn't the same as having one of our own.

'You've got a television?'

Mrs Lederman smiled and nodded. 'As soon as we're unpacked, you must come round and watch it with us.' She glanced at my mother. 'If that's all right, Mrs Read?'

'As long as she doesn't make a nuisance of herself,' said Mummy.

A nuisance of myself is exactly what I made during my remaining years in the Agapemone. Almost every evening I was home, I would make the short journey across the lawn, bang on the Ledermans' front door and be admitted to their snug little home. I wasn't the only one, I was to find out years later. The Ledermans had barely moved in when a newspaper reporter, the first of many, came knocking at their back door, which opened on to the back lane. 'He tried to get a scandalous story out of me about a revolving bed and the high jinks the old people had been up to. I knew nothing about the sect, but he didn't believe me, offering me money, so I gave him short shrift,' Mrs Lederman recalled. 'Looking at all the old folks on

Zimmer frames and crutches, it seemed a most unlikely situation.'

Hans and Trudel Lederman became my lodestar when it came to families. I had no idea how a normal family operated. They taught me. Even more importantly, they offered me friendship and affection. One night, we watched a television programme together about the terrible tragedy of the Holocaust, in which many of their relatives had died. It was graphic and the details leapt off the screen to envelop us in its chilling grotesqueness. I was horrified and wondered, as we gazed silently at the pictures of piles of skeletal bodies, what my hosts were thinking. Were they watching in fear of recognising a face? We didn't talk much that night but watching the programme in their company built on the belief I was subconsciously forming, that discrimination of any kind is deeply damaging and never justified.

I also learned about hope. How out of the ashes of their personal tragedy had risen a new family. Mr Lederman had a stepsister who was my age and whom he said might one day come and visit. Crossing the patch of lawn to the side door to my home that night, I found my mind in a jumble of emotion.

* * *

Uncle David had been away at sea for some weeks, so when I heard he was due home the evening after I arrived back from school for the holidays, I was delighted. He could be impatient and cross, but I knew he loved us dearly.

But this evening I was in for a surprise. Uncle David's Rolls-Royce swept up the drive just as Mummy was beginning to worry. Behind the car growled a motorbike, which screeched to a stop at the front door. A young man, clad entirely in black, alighted.

'Joe is staying the night,' my uncle explained to my mother. Joe was a member of the ship's crew, he said, who was on his way home.

I was impressed. How generous of my uncle. And how Christian for an officer to grant a mere rating a bed for the night. I stared at our hirsute tattooed guest as he and my uncle took their seats at my grandmother's dining table. I longed to ask Joe if he had sailed round Cape Horn (I was heavily into adventure stories at the time). But before I could summon up the courage, my mother shooed me off to bed, reminding me Margaret was due home from school the next day.

'If you don't get a good night's sleep, you'll be too tired to enjoy your sister's company,' she reminded me.

Over the years, an informal tradition had emerged. The morning after Uncle David arrived home from sea, Mummy always allowed me to carry up a cup of tea to his bedroom, so he could sleep in. But the following morning, when I presented myself to my mother ready for my chore, she had other ideas. 'Uncle David is sleeping in this morning and doesn't want to be disturbed,' she said.

'But I'm not going to disturb him. I always take him a cup of tea after he gets home.' I suddenly remembered our guest. 'I could take the sailor one, too.'

'That's very kind of you, Kitty, but not today,' my mother replied, giving no hint her decision was to protect me – and perhaps herself – from my inevitable questions had I been faced with the sight of two grown men sharing a bed. It was years before I would realise the situation – and marvel at my mother's quiet and tactful action.

* * *

I loved to lie on Eden's parquet floor, watching the dust dance in the sunlight streaming through the top of the chapel's arched windows where the shutters didn't reach. I would breathe in deeply, filling my lungs with the stale air heavy with the whiff of musty books and sawdust, which fell in tiny piles from the worm holes in the rows of upright chairs. Each chair had a little box fixed to its back in which a copy of the Agapemone hymnal, *Voice of the Bride*, lay ready – but never to be used again. Mixed in with the dust and must was the faint but distinct smell of damp. I had discovered a discoloured patch of wall in the little spider-infested room behind the pipe organ, where I also found a pile of volumes of my grandfather's sermons.

'I am my Beloved's and His desire is towards me,' I read as I flipped through his sermons, which were printed privately in 1927 following his death, entitled 'Extempore Addresses, Given during the years 1925, 1926, and 1927':

> She comes up from the wilderness of the world, from the trammel and the stress and the strife and the noise of the world; she comes up from the world leaning on her beloved, utterly dependent, hopeless in herself, but absolutely at rest, without fear, without doubt, without any uncertainty, she comes up from the wilderness leaning on her beloved and every moment nearing home.

'Yuck,' I muttered as I replaced the book back on the pile.

One day I came across a couple of old newspapers tucked away in the bottom drawer of the desk, including a black-bordered copy of *The Times*, dated Friday, 19 November 1852. The stiff cream-coloured pages crackled as I spread them on the floor and read about the state funeral of Arthur Wellesley, 1st Duke of Wellington. Tucked inside was a small pamphlet, entitled 'The Little Book Open: The Testimony of Br. Prince concerning what Jesus Christ has done by his Spirit to Redeem the Earth'. I had heard the old ladies sometimes talk about 'Brother Prince' and assumed this must be another name for my grandfather. 'No, Kitty, he wasn't your grandfather,' Waa had told me when I'd asked her. 'But, like your grandfather, he was a very wonderful man.'

The pamphlet told me little when I flipped through its pages of overblown language. I cast it aside. Little did I realise then that, 100 years before, it was this little privately printed booklet, more than any other publication, that had set the seal of scandal on the home in which I was growing up. And it was years before I was to learn that

Henry James Prince had been the founder of the Agapemone and that he had claimed to be a messenger sent by God to herald the Second Coming!

Ellen was one of the few people encouraged to enter Eden periodically, where she stirred the layers of dust settling on the heavy gold-leaf picture frames, the rows of hardback chairs and the Lalique vase set on a table next to the organ. The only other visitor was a Mr Mountford, who lived in the gatehouse and played the huge and valuable Willis pipe organ every week, until it was sold to a Roman Catholic church in Bedminster.

Watching these comings and goings, my sisters and I soon learned that the key to the chapel's arched-glass entrance door was hung on a hook high up on the wall of the chapel's small vestibule. It wasn't long before Margaret and I had invented several ways to pass a rainy afternoon, one of which involved sliding up and down the parquet floor of this ornate chapel-cum-Victorian living room. Over the years Eden had become the perfect indoor playground, one we kept to ourselves, suspecting that those in authority over us would be scandalised by such a profane use of what had once been the spiritual heart of the community.

So, when I decided to ask a school friend to stay for a couple of weeks one holiday, and one day it was raining, it was to Eden I turned when I had run out of other ways of amusing my guest. (Little did I appreciate, back then, how eagerly these invitations were sought by those friends' parents, curious to learn what lay behind the high stone walls of the notorious Agapemone.)

We had already exhausted my version of snakes and ladders. The old ladies had no idea they were involved in this game, as they slowly went about their daily tasks, emptying hot water bottles, filling tea kettles and accomplishing the myriad small tasks consuming daily life for the old and infirm. The aim was to make our way from the western end of the mansion to the baize door leading to Granny's End without being seen by any of them. In this I had the advantage, for I knew if we met Toto all we had to do was be absolutely silent because she couldn't see us. With Emily Hine, we had to be both silent and invisible to avoid detection, as this fierce old lady's five senses were all in good order. If either of us was spotted by these unsuspecting participants – usually with a polite 'Good morning, young lady' – it was back to the starting point to begin our journey all over again. However, I did have the sense not to involve my friends in another game which Margaret and I played: knocking on the old ladies' bedroom doors and then running away before they could get to the door and see us.

Pam, the first friend of several I invited to stay, was like me: skinny and tall for her age. She was also good at games, beating me in our endless matches of croquet played on the uneven upper lawn. Pam was also clever academically and a natural leader. Other friends included Diana, whose head for heights rivalled Margaret's. Unlike my sister, I had never possessed either a head for heights or an antenna for looming trouble. After one of Diana's visits, my mother threatened to refuse permission for any more friends to stay. Diana and I had been caught on the roof. Then there was Lesley, pretty and feminine, who came from a 'normal' family, a rarity at our school, which was the refuge of many children from dysfunctional backgrounds. Lesley's parents were happily married and ran a shop in Bridgwater.

But on that particular rainy afternoon with Pam, after all the old people had departed for their nap, we silently walked along the twisting, gloomy passage, past where my mother was resting, past the pantry where Ellen was having a quiet post-lunch cup of tea, to the chapel vestibule. I climbed on the little carved chair by the doors and reached up for the key.

'Are we allowed in here?' whispered Pam as I hopped down, inserted the key in the lock and flung open the stained-glass door.

'Not really,' I replied airily. 'But we often go in!'

My friend stared in awe – at the long, vaulted room with its arched windows; the rows of upright chairs with little boxes attached to their backs. And then wide-eyed at the incongruous scarlet sofas and whitewashed walls covered with oil paintings of cattle in gloomy Highland landscapes, framed in heavy gold leaf. 'Wow,' she whispered.

She took a tentative step forward towards the three shallow steps leading down to the far end, where a black and gold table stood on a raised dais. Her eyes widened as she saw the huge ornate stand, carved in the shape of an eagle with the Bible resting on the bird's outstretched wings.

'Olive, one of the old ladies you met at lunch, carved that,' I said.

I led my friend to the upright chairs, where we sat and wriggled, so I could illustrate to Pam how the rush seating made patterns on our thighs. She removed a hymn book from the back of the chair in front of her, opened it and glanced through its pages, wrinkling her nose in disgust before replacing it in its little box.

'All about love and brides,' she sniffed. I was glad I hadn't told her about my idea of taking one back to school so we could sing the hymns in chapel.

Next, Pam turned her attention to the rectangle marked out in dark wood on the floor in front of the dais. 'What's that, Kitty?' We scampered down the steps to stare at the gold plaque set near the far end of the rectangle.

'It's where my grandfather is buried.'

Pam leant forward, her long black plaits hanging. 'He's actually *buried* here? Like in Westminster Abbey? Like Henry VII?'

I nodded. Neither of us had ever been to Westminster Abbey, but we had studied Henry VII in history the previous term, so we knew where he was buried.

'Is it real gold?'

I had impressed Pam! This was going well. 'I think so.'

'What does it say? I.H.S. or is it J.H.S.?'

I didn't know. I.H.S. stood for In His Service and J.H.S. were my grandfather John Hugh Smyth-Pigott's initials, but I wasn't sure which was engraved in the gold.

'Your family must be awfully rich.'

'I don't think so,' I hedged. I thought of the fuss over the cheque-bouncing incident. I thought of my mother's having to get a job. It was time for a distraction.

Grabbing two cushions from the moth-eaten sofas, I threw one at Pam, shouting, 'Let's race.' Running to the back of the chapel, I called for her to follow before plonking myself down on my cushion just in front of the organ bench. Using my arms and legs, I began to propel myself forward as fast as I could. Pam was soon in hot pursuit. Faster and faster we slid, down the wide aisle between the chairs and bumping down the three shallow steps.

'First one to touch the dais wins,' I yelled as I rounded the edge of grandfather's grave and slid toward the dais. A quick glance over my shoulder saw Pam heading for the Bible stand. I reached the dais just as Pam rolled off her cushion to avoid crashing into it. She lay there staring up into the eagle's eyes.

'You look like its prey,' I yelled.

Pam began to wave her arms and legs as she squeaked like a frightened mouse. Soon we were both rolling with laughter on the floor.

'Kitty!' came a voice. 'What on earth do you think you're doing?'

My mother stood in the doorway. Her hair was all mussed and she had no lipstick on, signs we had woken her up from her afternoon nap. And if we had woken her, we could have also disturbed Granny. We could be in serious trouble.

'Just showing Eden to Pam.'

We scrambled to our feet, hiding the cushions behind our backs. Pam stifled a hiccup.

'And who gave you permission?'

'No one.'

'Put those back where they belong.' She was pointing to the cushions. 'And don't let me catch you in here again.'

That was as cross as my mother ever got and even that anger arose because of her concern that the old ladies would be very upset if they found out my friend and I had been playing in Eden. For the old ladies and probably for my mother – especially my fierce grandmother – Eden must have been a place of precious memories of happier and more secure times. It was certainly not an indoor playground.

Looking back, I realise my mother most likely had little energy left for anger. By 1952 all she could look forward to was her continuing daily struggle to keep the estate going until the last of her father's elderly followers had died.

As for the old ladies with whom I grew up, surely they could never let themselves believe that they had been deceived by my grandfather, even if, for some, disillusion stalked their darkest hours – as I believe it did for Emily. To have given up their lives for a spurious belief was a lot to acknowledge – and regret. But overall, Belovèd still seemed to stand tall and charismatic in their minds and emotions – even as recently as 20 years ago people who had known him still spoke of my grandfather with affection.

As a child I did not know enough to ask the old ladies the questions I wonder about now. Did they still cling to the hope that the time for Belovèd's recognition as the Messiah had not yet arrived? Or were there regrets because their Son of Man had been rejected by the world for the second time? Or, worst of all, had their belief in my grandfather long since died, leaving them to live out their lives in his crumbling community? But whatever their secret fears or worries, I believe the Abode of Love's elderly took comfort in the one promise Prince, and later my grandfather, had fulfilled: providing an earthly paradise, albeit an increasingly ramshackle one, where their every want was catered for.

How could my mother even contemplate leaving these vulnerable old people in the lurch? It was mainly on her shoulders that the well-being of these gentle and eccentric old ladies rested. No, her ambition was not for herself – it was too late for her, even though she was barely in her 40s – it was for us, her daughters. She desperately wanted to prevent the stigma that had haunted her life from blighting ours.

It was only gradually that I began to sense this. At first, it had seemed more hinted at than real, like the ghost said to haunt the long upstairs passage. But someone had thought we were 'peculiar'; we seemed rich but weren't. And why were all these old people living with my grandmother anyway? I was growing increasingly puzzled.

But my fascination with Eden never left me. As a teenager, grappling with the confusion and embarrassment that followed my discovery of the truth about our strange home, I found comfort in its moth-eaten serenity. I used to spend hours there, daydreaming my family was 'ordinary', and lived in a council house and washed in the kitchen sink. And it was Eden, which looked like a place of worship yet at the same time seemed more like a drawing room, which encapsulated the apocalyptic millenarian religious sect which lasted for just over a century before fading into oblivion.

12

The Great Manifestation

Hepworth Dixon, distinguished traveller and editor of *The Athenaeum*, had heard of the Abode of Love long before he visited in the 1860s to investigate the strange community for his two-volume *Spiritual Brides*. He was the only journalist ever to be granted an interview. For years, newspapers had been drooling over tales of the elevation of attractive young ladies within the community, of reports of its strange leader having 'brides of the week' and of the vicious bloodhounds believed to roam the grounds ready to attack intruders. They had reported with glee when Brother Prince paraded through the Great Exhibition of 1851 in an ornate carriage once owned by the Dowager Queen Adelaide. But nothing was to compare with the Great Manifestation of 1856.

The previous ten years had proved a difficult decade for the Abode of Love. In 1848, Agnes Thomas had claimed, during the civil case disputing her sister Louisa's return to the community from a lunatic asylum, that Prince was unfit to be entrusted with Louisa's care as he and the wife of his loyal lieutenant, Reverend Samuel Starky, lived in adultery – he had been spotted leaving her bedroom. This assertion started another flurry of newspaper inches devoted to the strange community buried in rural Somerset. The local *Bridgwater Times* reported how 'pretty laundresses' were being raised above their station and paraded in silks and satins along the terrace – the same terrace where I would ride my bicycle.

Then there was the story of how Prince chose his 'bride of the week' from a revolving stage on which sat the prospective young women with Prince at their centre. The brides' husbands – where there were any – would push the stage until it began revolving at high speed, at which point the husbands would retire. The woman who faced Prince when the stage slowed to a stop became his bride of the week. I wish I could write that I had seen evidence of a stage, let alone a revolving one – nothing was ever discarded in my childhood home – but I never did.

The newspaper tales energised families of the believers, who pleaded with their loved ones to abandon this den of iniquity. Some former believers needed no urging: the widow of a prosperous grocery-business owner ran away from the Abode of Love and when tracked down by zealous believers refused to get out of her bed, even in the face of eternal damnation. A local lawyer, who had joined the Abode of Love with his wife but seen the error of his ways, escaped by scaling the walls – but when he returned to rescue his wife, she showed little interest in defecting.

Worse still were the suicides. One devout believer, suffering from a psychiatric illness, was found hanging from a tree. Another, a tax collector from Dorset, cut his throat after too much 'soul-destroying dogma of the notorious Prince', according to the local newspaper. And a wealthy farmer, who had given his all to Abode of Love coffers, tried to take his own life but ended up in an asylum.

Something had to be done to stop the haemorrhaging besides the seemingly futile attempts to convince the strayed to return.

The 'Great Manifestation of God's Love for Humanity' took place in late 1855 or early 1856. In his self-published pamphlet of that year,

'The Little Book Open, The Testimony of Brother Prince concerning what Jesus Christ has done by his Spirit to Redeem the Earth', Prince promised to finally overcome the flesh. The living would be saved, the flesh liberated from sin and made perfect in this world rather than having to wait until the next. To achieve 'flesh made perfect', and despite the fact that he was still married and his wife was alive and well, Prince proclaimed he must experience sexual union with a woman – and a virgin, at that. By this act, he claimed he would complete man's salvation and reconciliation with God! He would conquer death and sweep away sin. It was a bizarre argument, given that during both his legal marriages – first to Martha and secondly to Julia – he had denied himself and his wives any physical union. Those two marriages could be said to be truly 'in spirit' only.

This 'spiritual' marriage was most certainly nothing of the kind. The resident virgins were in a paroxysm of excitement. Who was to be the lucky lady? Prince wasn't giving anything away.

At last, the day of the Great Manifestation dawned. His wife and followers assembled in Eden. As Prince entered they burst forth in song:

> *All Hail, thou King of Glory, now*
> *Thy love their homage brings*
> *Now waits until the nations bow*
> *But crowns thee King of Kings.*

According to an enduring legend, Prince, dressed in a scarlet velvet robe, took his seat on his throne between his 'two candlesticks', as the Reverend and Mrs Starky were affectionately known. Prince's 'bride', believed to be Anne Willett Patterson, a beautiful young servant who had lived with her mother and three sisters in the community for some years, then made her appearance wearing a dress of white Honiton lace with a long train and decked in gold.

The two consummated their union on a scarlet-covered table serving as an altar. This act of depravity, a parody of the Book of

Revelations 19:7, 8, 9, was supposed to have been witnessed by Prince's legal wife, plus 12 men dressed in black and an equal number of women in white, as well as the congregation.

Did it happen like that? Certainly Prince, at 45, was still as obsessed with the Song of Solomon as he had been as a teenager. He was probably still sexually vigorous, with a wife many years his senior. And, increasingly, he fell prey to the charms of nubile young women. But claims that he had indulged in sexual intercourse in public have always been fiercely disputed by community members. Those who would have been eyewitnesses to the Great Manifestation were long gone to their heavenly reward by the time my sisters and I arrived to live in the Abode of Love. And, mercifully, we had grown up and moved away by the time we even learned such juicy titbits. But that didn't stop us, as adults, attempting to find out the truth.

'It's awful to tell lies, like having a mistress on the altar. It just shows they don't know what they're talking about,' said Great Aunt Tup.

Contemporary newspaper accounts refer only to adultery and not an act of what would surely have been gross indecency in the burgeoning Victorian age. The prosecuting counsel of the ongoing *Nottridge* v. *Prince* lawsuit didn't make a single reference to sexual irregularities. Even Hepworth Dixon, writing a mere ten years later, appears to assume that while the 'marriage' had been public, consummation was private.

One day in early June 1856 and probably not long after the Great Manifestation, Elizabeth Maber's sister, Mary, was found missing. She was eventually discovered two miles away drowned in a pond popular with the community for bathing. The only clue to her state of mind is a cryptic suicide note:

> This is a day of judgment to me and fearful perplexity – when I go – Self will go from the abode – if my wretched heart were not stone and unbelieving – what [Prince] said would have relieved me.

Newspaper accounts on the resulting inquest speculated whether she had suffered from 'softening of the brain' or was upset by the elevation of servants above ladies such as herself. She had certainly been depressed for some time over her loss of faith, perhaps due to the knowledge that a young niece of hers was dying – in vivid contrast to her leader's promises of paradise and eternal life.

But perhaps recent events had proved the final straw for a sheltered and impressionable young woman, as had been the case with the Reverend Lewis Price, one of the original Lampeter brethren who left the community in disgust only to return a couple of years later with a mob which scaled the walls in search for his wife Harriet. Eventually, Harriet was discovered, not in the community but in Salisbury, a cathedral city some distance away. The couple were briefly reconciled, and Harriet spent the rest of her life hoping to be recaptured and taken back to the Abode of Love.

The Great Manifestation cost Brother Prince dear. Things went from bad to worse when it became only too apparent that his 'spiritual bride' was pregnant. Prince was forced to adjust his doctrine, preaching that the birth of his daughter Eva was a last gasp by Satan. He sent his aging lieutenants out proselytising in nearby towns, but with little success. The meetings were well attended, but by sceptics who brought each one to a speedy conclusion with their booing and hissing.

By 1868, when Hepworth Dixon received permission to interview Prince and his faithful, he found about 60 middle-aged men and women living apparently harmoniously on the spacious and luxurious estate. He was invited into Eden – part chapel with its arched windows, part comfortable sitting room with its scarlet velvet sofas, part games room, with its billiard table and rack of cues flanking a symbol of the Lamb and the Dove. While he waited for Prince to appear, Dixon was offered biscuits and his choice of dry sherry or sweet port, both of excellent quality. Eventually, Prince entered, flanked by two beautiful women, and took his seat at the centre of a semicircle of 'saints'.

Dixon was told the faithful knew 'no craving after devil's love', with the result no children were born. But what about the child I have seen playing outside, he asked. Ah, replied Prince, the child was living witness to the last great triumph of the devil in man. The bizarre explanations continued. None of the faithful expected to die and dismissed those who had as sinners.

'Do you teach?' asked Dixon.

'No,' they replied.

Did they perhaps preach, read, farm, feed the poor?

The faithful, it seemed, did very little. Dixon concluded they had given up attempting to change mankind, and perhaps in an echo of Prince's early religious training were content to drink good sherry and play billiards while they waited to be swept up to their heavenly reward.

13

Christmas at the 'A'

John Victor Read died suddenly at 11.15 p.m. at
Abingdon, Berks, aged 66.

Entry in the Agapemone diary for
Tuesday, 21 October 1952

My mother sat at my grandfather's kneehole desk, pen in hand. Before her lay several sheets of heavy cream paper, some covered in her handwriting, the top one half-full. By her hand sat the heavy iron stamp she had used to emboss our address at the top right-hand corner of the paper. A shiny black, its swirling gold-leaf decoration, painted by Olive many years before, was beginning to flake.

'I'm just writing to Granny May, and to your father, to say how sorry I am about Grandpa John,' she explained.

'Did you like him?'

'Yes, Kitty, I was always fond of John – or Pops, as we called him.'

So had I been. I cried when I was told he had died – and on holiday. I wondered what it would be like to stay with Granny May and her sister without Grandpa John's leavening presence.

'Do you like Granny May?' I asked.

'She certainly didn't want me to marry her favourite son.'

'Why not, when she had lived here and knew everyone so well?'

'I don't think she felt I was good enough for him.' Unexpectedly, my mother's face lit up with the mischievous grin I glimpsed only too rarely. 'But then would anyone have been good enough for her precious Polo?'

She returned to her letters, drying the ink with the Victorian silver rocker-blotter, which lay on the desk next to a photograph of my mother's father as a pious-looking young seminarian. It was an unthreatening picture, one in which I noticed how my mother had inherited her father's aristocratic nose and mouth. One day, when I began to appreciate the finer points of male beauty, I would realise how sensual was the shape of his lips.

'He was very good-looking, wasn't he?' commented my mother as she folded her letters and placed them carefully in their envelopes. 'You would have loved him, Kit. And he would have adored the three of you.'

I perched on the edge of the sofa, pleased with the idea and also enjoying my mother's company before she made her first daily visit to the pub, and before Uncle Pat turned up to fill the house with his loud voice and tuneless whistling.

My glance flickered over the other items lying on the desk: the maroon leather-bound Agapemone diary and the Victorian calendar, the small box with the month, day and date showing through three windows in its carved wooden front. It was Ellen's job first thing every morning, when she drew back the heavy brocade curtains and lit the fire, to change the day and date by turning the little carved knobs on one side of the box. (This calendar now sits on my mantel.) And the handmade pewter frame hung to one side, with the Latin saying '*Homo sum; humani nil a me alienum puto*' painstakingly engraved in Gothic script. I had asked my Latin teacher to translate it for me the previous term – I said I had found it in a book. 'I am a man; I count nothing human alien from me,' she'd told me. I had been rather disappointed.

My mother and I weren't often on our own. Now that she was working I rarely saw her during the day, and in the evenings, when she settled down with her whisky and her library book, I fled her thickened, over-careful enunciation and need to put out a hand to steady herself when she rose from her chair. Instead I would go to the Ledermans' welcoming cottage; perhaps I should have stayed home more often. Surely, in those long hours before bedtime, with my mother's tongue loosened by her pre-dinner drink, her wine with supper and her postprandial whisky, I could have unlocked the enigma of my childhood home; especially during the long, lonely months when my uncle was at sea.

I was surprised at my pleasure at being alone with her that morning – and unlikely to be interrupted: Granny's nose was being dressed by the visiting nurse and Waa was mending my brand-new school tunic, which I had snagged on a hook the evening before.

'But why weren't you good enough for Daddy?' I was genuinely puzzled. 'Granny May had only been a KP, after all.'

My mother smiled. 'It was nothing to do with class, Kitty. It was to do with your grandfather. She didn't get on with him . . .'

'But . . .'

'She didn't want any of her precious sons to have anything to do with us.' I heard a surprising and unaccustomed bitterness enter my mother's tone. 'So your father and I eloped!'

I felt my jaw drop. 'You eloped?'

'Yes.'

'Whatever did Granny say?'

'There wasn't much she could say! She was in no position—' She clammed up.

'What do you mean, she was in no position?'

But my mother would say no more.

A couple of days later, I asked my grandmother what she had thought of my father's father. I was never to pluck up the courage to question her about the man I knew as her own husband. I don't know why; perhaps I sensed she wouldn't tell me. Or would get upset. The very worst crime in my childhood home was to 'upset your grandmother'. I never dared. But I reckoned my father's father was a safe subject.

'It's sad about Grandpa John, isn't it, Granny?'

'Yes, it is, Kitty.'

'Did you know him well?'

'Yes, he was a very nice, polite young man.' She paused, adding quietly, as if unable to help herself, 'That tiresome young May did very well for herself!'

* * *

It wasn't long after Christmas that year that I would begin to solve the mystery surrounding Grandpa John's family. Christmases at the 'A', as I came to call my childhood home, were truly memorable – on a scale, I understand, with my grandfather's own birthday celebrations on the 1st of August. The estate would be filled with visitors: my cousins and aunt from Holford, elderly followers from London; sometimes even visitors from Norway, where a small group of followers still lived. During one of these celebrations, largely unchanged since the community's heydays, I received a complete beaded outfit from these kind people.

On Christmas Eve, Granny would walk through the mansion carrying a copper warming pan filled with incense. (I only remember the latter days, when her sight had gone and she was forced to make her annual progress with the assistance of one of her sons, or her daughter.) How the scent lingered in the long corridors and hid in long-shut-up bedrooms, and filled our nostrils when Margaret and I ventured in for a spot of rooting, sometimes months later – even now, incense conjures up not a high Mass or the hippie '60s but childhood memories.

Edward would erect the huge Christmas tree in the withdrawing area of the dining room. It was a branch from one of the cedars that dotted the grounds – the only tree to escape such severe pruning was Granny's blue cedar. We children would help decorate the tree with our own creations and antique decorations, such as the glass birds with real feathers for tails, remnants of another era.

As soon as we woke on Christmas morning, we were allowed to open our stockings: calf-length school socks which had been hung empty at the end of our beds and had overnight magically filled with erasers, marbles and always a gold-covered chocolate in the toe. Each small gift was wrapped in paper which had been carefully refolded after use the previous year. But we had to wait until the early evening to open the bulk of our presents.

Later in the morning, if Uncle David was at home, he would take Mummy into town to the Catholic Mass. But there was no religious celebration in the community and Eden remained shut up.

Christmas lunch was also the one occasion of the year when Granny would preside over the meal, sitting regally at the head of the table, back straight, chiffon veil flowing over her shoulders. Every seat at the long dining table was taken. Uncle David, seated at the end next to his mother, would carve an enormous turkey, hacking at it impatiently, unlike his brother sitting at the foot of the long table: Uncle Pat would carve his haunch of beef with meticulous skill, the slices as thin as the leaves of a book.

Following lunch, the agonising wait for presents continued, although they were rarely a surprise to Margaret and me, as they had been placed under the tree days before, giving us plenty of opportunity to creep in and feel through the paper.

But, at last, everyone would assemble around the tree and Granny would cut off the presents, one by one, with her scissors, handing them to us to distribute. Only after everyone had received theirs could we open ours.

That Christmas I began to wonder whether I hadn't been forgotten – by my mother, of all people – until she took me by the hand and led me to the stables, followed by as many old ladies as could make the walk. The little procession reached the end stall where a skewbald pony with a wayward stick-up mane gave us all a knowing look.

'Happy Christmas, Kit,' she said.

'He's mine?' I couldn't believe it. 'All mine?'

The assembled throng nodded in unison. I wondered briefly why I hadn't guessed something was up when I had come across Edward clearing all the old lawnmowers and bath chairs and painting easels from the stall in the middle of winter. And I was amazed Margaret hadn't told me. But, at 16, her sights were set on a future of art college and painting; she no longer had much interest in riding. Perhaps she also felt that my having a pony would ease her own inevitable departure from home.

Returning to school after Christmas was agony. We weren't allowed to bring our own ponies until we had reached what the school regarded as the responsible age of 12. I begged for an early weekend home and could barely contain myself during the inevitable wait for my mother. We arrived home so late Mummy insisted I leave seeing Pinto until the next morning.

'There's a gale blowing in, Kit,' she warned. But the temptation was too great and as soon as I heard her snoring, I slipped into a sweater and jodhpurs and headed for the stables.

A sudden gust of cold wind almost tore the handle of the side door from my grasp. Clouds raced across the moon as I stepped outside. One second I was in a huge, black inky space and the next the whole garden was moonlit. I felt an unusual tremor of fear. I glanced at my watch: nearly midnight. The big cedar on the upper lawn sighed as the wind caught it, sending the swing moving as though propelled by a ghost. The bushes bordering the path up to the balustrade swayed like a crowd.

It took all my courage to ease myself through the squeaky gate into the shadowy courtyard of the stables, but the sound of distant stamping drew me on. I eased the door into the stable block and was rewarded with the heady smell of warm horseflesh. I could just make out Pinto's white patches in the darkness as he turned toward me.

'Cup, cup, Pinto,' I whispered, holding a biscuit stolen from the supper table in my outstretched hand. 'Good boy! I couldn't wait till morning to see you.'

The bristles on his nose tickled my palm as he took the biscuit in his yellow teeth and then searched for more, nudging me back against the wall with his nose. 'Hey, clumsy! Don't be greedy.'

I stopped, jolted into silence by the unmistakable squeak of the stable gate, followed by the sound of heavy boots on the cobblestone stableyard. I crept under my pony's neck and stood rooted to the spot with fear as the stable door opened. A beam of light flashed round the huge space and came to a stop at Pinto. I ducked lower and wished my heart wasn't making such a noise.

'This is the police. Show yourself,' commanded a voice from beyond the light.

I ducked back under my pony's neck so the intruder could see me.

'You're one of Mrs Smyth's granddaughters.' The torch was lowered and I could make out the tall helmeted figure of the village policeman. 'What are you doing out here, miss, in the middle of the night?'

'I came to see my pony. Did someone call you?'

'No, miss. We've been patrolling round here for close on 50 years, I'd say; since old Mr Read was attacked, anyways.'

Old Mr Read attacked? When? Why? My mind raced as the policeman escorted me back to the side door and made me promise not to sneak out after dark again, 'Or I'll consider it my duty to inform your grandmother, young lady,' he'd said. As I crept up the stairs to my bedroom, I wondered who to ask.

'You'd be better asking someone else about such things,' said Edward when I tackled him the next morning. He attached the hosepipe to a tap. 'If you've got nothing better to do, can you help me wash down the floor of the conservatory?'

Next, I tried Waa. But she too demurred. 'It was all a long, long time ago, Kitty, and such a difficult time.'

So I tackled my mother. 'Who told you about anyone being attacked?' she asked, staring at me suspiciously.

'I just heard it,' I lied. 'I can't remember where.'

'It happened before I was born,' she replied.

'But what happened?'

'Your great-grandfather, Charles Stokes Read, was attacked.'

'But why?'

My mother sighed. 'They were after your grandfather – my father.'

'But—'

'Who knows, Kit!'

Could this be the 'incident' my paternal grandparents had alluded to? The one which led to my great-grandfather's early death? I resolved to find out. But I would have to tread carefully if I were to get anyone to tell me about it.

'Lettit,' I began casually a couple of days later – once again, I was perched on the window sill in the laundry: Cissy had gone into town, leaving Lettit on her own, and vulnerable to my questions – 'it must have been awful when "old Mr Read" was attacked.'

'Oh, it was, my dear,' she replied. 'We were all scared to death. So many people didn't try to understand what a good man your grandfather was. There was a lot of misunderstanding back then.' She shook her head in sorrow.

'But it was my great-grandfather, not Belovèd, who was attacked, wasn't it?'

She nodded. 'Yes, it was.'

'But why?' I asked again.

But I was to get nowhere with my questions. The more I asked Lettit, the more flustered she became. 'You must ask your mother. It isn't my place,' she said finally.

I tried another tack.

'Was Granny May still living here?'

'Yes, dear,' she admitted.

I decided to stretch the few facts I had learned. 'She told me my great-grandfather died because of the attack.'

'It certainly contributed, of that I'm sure,' she replied. 'And now I must get on, this ironing won't do itself.'

14

A Tarring and Feathering

My paternal great-grandfather's steadfast support of my grandfather had already cost Charles Stokes Read dear. He had been brought in as a director of the Vis Vitae Bread Company of London and was also a member of an influential club when he and Reverend Pigott met as recruits in the Salvation Army. The two men immediately hit it off. Just two years apart in age, perhaps it was their differences that drew them together: the clean-shaven, charismatic younger son with no family money but a romantic, adventuring background and the bearded, wealthy London merchant and paterfamilias. When they met, Charles was a pillar of the upper middle class with eight equally prosperous siblings and a brood of children that would, in time, increase to nine.

Within months of joining the Salvation Army, Charles and Sarah had donated the family jewels, followed by increasingly large donations of cash. This largesse came to an abrupt end when 'major' Pigott resigned rather than be drummed out of the Army. Charles and Sarah had left immediately too, taking with them a small group of well-heeled former Salvationists – but leaving their donated money behind.

Over the next few years, Charles and Sarah would continue to pay for their close ties to my grandfather. Charles was fired from the bread company, blackballed by his club and ostracised by his brothers and sisters, who decided he was mad. In the early 1900s, he was forced to retire, and moved those of his family who were willing to come to the Abode of Love, now led by my grandfather. Charles's two eldest sons and his eldest daughter turned their backs on their parents.

* * *

Why a reporter from the *Daily Mail* was skulking outside the notorious Abode of Love that particular Sunday evening of 7 November 1908 has never been established. The editor would vociferously deny the paper had been tipped off about what was about to happen, but there his reporter was, admiring the 'picture of rest and peace in its beautiful rural surroundings' on that unusually mild Sunday evening. He noted how at five-thirty exactly lights shone through the Gothic windows of the strange community's chapel; at six the sound of women's voices raised in song floated towards him; and at seven, how all became silent and dark once again.

The reporter was just about to leave when he heard the sound of a car approaching. He watched a huge vehicle stop just before it reached the community's locked gates and discharge four men, who began walking up and down outside the community. The reporter approached the vehicle. He saw several men still inside, one of them in a policeman's uniform. He glimpsed a policeman's helmet and an inspector's cap. He asked if they were going to the Abode of Love, and if so, why?

When they didn't answer, the reporter returned to his spot beneath the community's protective high stone wall and watched as the vehicle drove past him again and on to the Abode gates, finally turning into the yard of the Lamb Inn, the public house hard by the community wall.

Unaware of what was going on outside, the faithful spilled out into the corridors and passages as Eden emptied. At that point, one of the Kitchen Parlour approached Charles's 27-year-old daughter Millicent – someone had tapped on the window of the music room.

Curious, Millicent followed the woman outside just in time to glimpse three men moving through the dark gardens. The women hurried back into the house and told Charles. Sarah begged her husband not to go out, but he brushed her hand from his arm and disappeared through the front door. He had barely reached the stableyard before three men jumped him from behind. Two held him while the third produced a policeman's helmet filled with hot sticky tar mixed with feathers, and rammed it down over his head. As Charles stumbled about in shock and fear, one of the men who had been holding him clouted the top of the helmet, trying to force it over his eyes. His attackers then seized the frightened and bewildered man and began to drag him toward some bushes. Just then, Millicent ran up, with her mother in hot pursuit.

Hearing their voices, Charles, fearing for their safety, shouted for them to go away. The two women refused. 'If you go away, we will take no more notice of it,' Sarah called out to the men.

The intruders took off over the wall as Millicent pulled the helmet from her father's head. His hair was matted with tar and had feathers stuck in it. Streaks of black ooze ran down his cheeks and into his moustache and beard.

Other community members rushed up. One ran to fetch the local constable. Two began helping Charles back to the house. And then there came the sound of someone climbing back over the wall. A man, dressed as a policeman, dropped down into the darkened garden. It was Michael Sale, one of the men charged with tarring and feathering my great-grandfather. He was presumably dressed as a policeman to disguise himself.

'I dare you to arrest me,' he proclaimed as he was seized.

He was held until the village constable arrived. Police Constable Catley asked the intruder why he was in the grounds.

'I came to tar and feather old Pigott,' he replied. He went on to state that when he hadn't been able to spot Pigott quickly, he had decided to attack the first representative of 'the beastly place' he came across.

Michael Ormerod Sale, an advertising agent of Eaton Terrace, and his accomplices in the attack, grocer Foster John Pinnall of Camberwell and labourer John Green of Holborn, were quickly taken to the police cells in nearby Bridgwater, where they were charged with assaulting Charles Stokes Read and being on enclosed premises for an unlawful purpose.

The following morning, the streets around the town courthouse were in chaos as the locals fought for admittance and a glimpse of the injured man and his wife as they arrived to give evidence. Charles, looking shaken, his face burned from the tar, and his hair, moustache and beard ragged from where the tar had had to be cut out, limped slowly to the entrance, his wife on his arm. Sarah carried a picnic basket. Once inside, she insisted on taking the basket down to the cells, where she distributed sandwiches and a hot drink to the three men accused of attacking her husband.

In court, the ringleader, Sale, testified that he had planned the whole thing, including recruiting his accomplices, with the sole purpose of teaching 'old Smyth-Pigott' a lesson. Pinnall and Green said Sale had simply invited them on an 'outing' and that they had no idea what had been planned.

The magistrates found Sale guilty of assault and trespass, and sentenced him to one calendar month's imprisonment with hard labour. Pinnall and Green were found guilty of trespass and fined £5 each. With no hope of finding such a large sum, Sale's accomplices joined him in the cells for a month's hard labour.

The effect on the community was devastating. It seemed

incomprehensible to these gentle people that they could be so hated. In the years that followed, resentment grew between the Read family and that of Belovèd over the way Charles had unwittingly become a scapegoat for his leader – until, during my childhood, the Reads' resentment had grown to include even the silver Charles had brought to Somerset.

But, as so often happens in these situations, the attack on such a kindly and gentle man forged ties between the Agapemone and the village of Spaxton that were never loosened. The village already benefited from the community's continuing largesse – annual deliveries of coal and joints of beef, plus the dried once-used tea leaves. In the wake of the attack on my great-grandfather, the village became the community's unofficial security.

My mother told me of one occasion when she had been enjoying her lunchtime drink in the Lamb Inn when a curious reporter had dropped in, eager for titillating details of the strange community next door. 'You got me there,' the landlord replied, scratching his head perplexed. 'We never see sight nor sound of any of them.' His reply was echoed by a chorus of muttered 'Aye's from the little group of farm labourers hunched over a game of dominoes and pints of scrumpy cider.

15

A Birth and a Death

Dora died at 1.30 a.m. in Minehead Nursing Home.

Entry in the Agapemone diary for
Saturday, 10 January 1953

I grew surprisingly close to my mother that year, to the extent of sleeping in the second bed in her large bedroom next door to Katie's Room, at the west end of the mansion. I had a perfectly good bedroom of my own, but now Margaret was there only infrequently and the courage I got from her proximity in the next room had fled as the huge house grew emptier with each of my visits. I had grown so used to sleeping in a dormitory containing upwards of a dozen girls, I found the silence unnerving. So I took to creeping down to my mother's room on the floor below and sliding into the second bed there. Eventually, she got one of the KP to make up the other bed permanently.

But there were disadvantages to sharing a room with my mother: she snored. So did Gay, who slept on an old chaise longue at the other side of the room. I soon found if I wasn't asleep by the time the pair of them came to bed, it would be hours before tiredness shut out the constant rumble.

* * *

The previous year, Trudel Lederman had given birth to a daughter and named her Ruth. My grandmother had been ecstatic. 'Come, give me your arm,' she had commanded my mother one morning. Together, the two walked up the long, tiled passage, past the kitchens towards the side door, which I used every evening to visit the little family in the trim cottage across the lawn. As my grandmother made her slow, careful way through the mansion accompanied by my mother, heads popped out of rooms to stare in amazement at the unaccustomed sight.

'We're going to visit the baby,' my mother explained as they passed.

'They have named her Ruth, after me,' added my grandmother proudly.

Not strictly true, but who's quibbling?

Slowly they made their way across the grass.

'You can go now, Lavita,' she said as they neared the Ledermans' front door, which had been flung open in welcome by Trudel.

The baby, as all babies were in those days, had been placed outside in her pram, covered with netting to keep away the sundry cats which roamed the estate. After exchanging smiles of understanding with Trudel, my mother dropped back to join me. Together, we watched Granny approach the pram. Trudel removed the netting and my grandmother bent to inspect the tiny sleeping girl, reaching out a tentative finger to the infant's downy cheek.

It wasn't the last time my grandmother went to see the baby and her visits revealed a tender, loving side to the fierce woman who headed the community. They also had a subtle impact on the community's acceptance of the young strangers and within days there was a constant stream of elderly women admiring the tiny figure in the pram.

Baby Ruth was also a magnet for Waa. She loved babies, having raised two generations of children that were not hers. 'They were such beautiful children,' she would tell me, referring to her first generation of charges, my mother and two uncles. 'I could hardly believe it when

Belovèd called me into his study one day and asked me to be David's nurse.' She had cared for the baby boy as if he were hers, watching over him every second of the day, sleeping in his nursery at night.

What she didn't tell me was how, shortly after David's birth had been registered by the local registrar, Waa had unwisely ventured outside the community. She had no idea the registrar had been interviewed by a local newspaper about his visit to the notorious Agapemone, so she had set off, pushing the baby in his carriage, down a local lane. She had gone barely 100 yards when she found herself surrounded by a crowd of reporters, yelling questions at her about the baby's parentage. The young nanny from this enclosed community had no idea that the birth of her charge would have scandalised society – and galvanized the press, both national and local. Editors had sent their star reporters down to hunt out the latest titbits about a community that had been making headlines for 50 years. Frightened, but determined they would not get close to David, Waa turned her back on them and scuttled to the safety of the mansion, pushing the pram before her.

The next day, yet another story appeared in the newspaper. Accompanying the article was a drawing of the back view of a young Edwardian woman pushing a pram, her face half-turned in anxiety.

Waa loved to tell me stories of when my mother and uncles were children. Even a quick glimpse at the youngest member of the Lederman family was enough to jog her memories of life in the Agapemone long ago – how David hated picnics but would endure them, and how one day Pat had ridden his bicycle down the terrace at top speed, crashing through the china and sandwiches just as she had laid out the children's picnic. 'Oh, he was a naughty boy. But it was just devilment. There was no malice in him,' she laughed indulgently. And she would tell me of brushing Lavita's long black hair with 100 strokes each night and how it grew so long that Lavita could sit on it.

One morning, even Emily Hine inched her way across the lawn to pronounce that she was aghast at the way Ruth's mother put the baby outside in her pram in all weathers. She told Trudel it wasn't healthy

135

to expose such a small baby to so much fresh air. Trudel listened politely and continued the practice. Eventually, after a few days of muttering, Emily gave up criticising.

* * *

I was due to take tea with Emily and, as usual, I had a question. I had overheard Uncle David and my mother discussing how they had wanted Ann to be a debutante. A debutante? I had only a vague idea of what debutantes were.

'Were you ever a debutante, Emily?' I asked when we were settled with our tea and stale arrowroot biscuits.

'No, Kitty. I was never pretty and I wouldn't have liked all those parties.' She smiled. 'I'm afraid I was rather a disappointment to my dear parents.'

'Why, if you were a nurse?'

'No one wanted to marry me.' She paused to take a sip of tea. 'But I didn't care for marriage. Then I met your grandfather.'

'Where did you meet him?'

'He was preaching in his London church and he seemed to be speaking to me alone.' She smiled again and her eyes grew dreamy. Somewhere a clock chimed the half-hour. There was a gurgle from her radiator, as the huge boiler sent water coursing through the system, trapping a myriad air bubbles. 'And so here I am.'

'But you took tea with Queen Victoria,' I urged, 'so you would know about debutantes.'

Emily looked suspicious. 'Why are you so anxious to know about debutantes, young lady?'

'Mummy and Uncle David wanted Ann to be presented at court,' I said.'

'What nonsense!' the old lady burst out.

I was taken aback. 'Ann would make a very good debutante,' I replied. 'She's beautiful and she loves clothes.'

'Your mother and uncle know perfectly well none of you girls can be debutantes. Goodness knows, they've been enough of a disappoint—'

She stopped and shot me a look.

'Besides, your parents are divorced. The King and Queen won't have anything to do with anybody who has a divorce in the family. And quite right too.' She reached for her gold-topped cane and thumped the carpet, as if summoning a servant.

'Well, I think it's pretty unkind.' It was becoming increasingly obvious my parents' divorce was why we were so 'peculiar', to quote Ann's former boyfriend. 'It's not our fault.'

* * *

I hadn't heard about the passing of 'dear Dora' until I came home for the Easter holidays and then it was only a passing remark between Uncle David and Mummy about the cost of funerals.

'Who's dead?' I asked.

The two glanced at me. 'Dora Beddow,' replied Uncle David.

'Did I know her?'

'It was long before your time,' replied my uncle.

I ran through the list of old ladies I lived with. The name didn't ring a bell. 'So, she didn't live here?'

'No,' my uncle answered shortly.

A couple of evenings later I lay in bed listening for the approach of Mummy's footsteps, followed by the tap, tap of Gay's long nails on the linoleum edging the Indian rug which ran the length of the upstairs passage.

'Mummy,' I called, as her shadow darkened the doorway.

'You should be asleep,' she replied.

'Tell me about the violet seller.'

My mother could never resist her oft-told tale about the coloured sketch of a Victorian violet-seller which hung on her bedroom wall.

The young girl is leaning forward, offering her bunch of violets, eyes huge and soulful beneath her tumble of dark hair. Once again she told me how her father had gone to London on a visit and come across the picture in a shop in Cheapside. 'It reminded him so much of me that he bought it and brought it home.'

She loved the picture, especially as her father had arrived with it at a difficult time, after her mother had accused her of 'looking like a little red Indian', with her long, straight black hair – which was not meant as a compliment. The picture now hangs in my home.

But that night I had an ulterior motive: I wanted to know more about Dora and had learnt that the circuitous route was the best way to get information. 'Why didn't Dora Beddow live here?'

'It was all a long time ago, Kitty. And it's long past your bedtime.'

* * *

It was Dora Beddow's mother, Rebecca, who first became enamoured with my grandfather – and perhaps also of his teachings. Rebecca's husband, Frederick, was a wealthy industrialist and accountant from the English Midlands who had helped set up the Vis Vitae Bread Company in London as a way of diversifying his now-considerable wealth. But the company, founded around 1887, had soon run into financial difficulties and Frederick Beddow, as a member of the board of directors, had proposed Charles Stokes Read as a new director to help the company regain its financial health. That decision was to have catastrophic consequences for Mr Beddow.

Rebecca Beddow soon struck up a friendship with Sarah Read. She went with Sarah and Charles to hear the dashing Reverend Pigott preach in various rented halls and, like so many women living at the dawn of the twentieth century, Mrs Beddow sensed that for all her worldly goods something was missing from her life. She was bored and dissatisfied but, unlike other women who were beginning to question their lack of rights, had no interest in women's suffrage.

Reverend Pigott gave her life meaning. He promised her salvation and fulfilment. The simple message, couched in convoluted and colourful language studded with references to the erotic Song of Solomon, soon had her spellbound. And for a woman of her class and attitude, she saw that by her association with the Reads, she had also found entrée to an inner circle whose members included wives of members of parliament. She also found the Reverend Pigott attractive.

At first, Frederick, as so many husbands before and since, was merely relieved his wife had found some way of occupying herself and their musically inclined daughter Dora. Dora, by now in her teens, had become so accomplished on the piano that Dear Belovèd asked her to accompany his services. Soon, Frederick found himself and his younger child, Arnold, helping to distribute Agapemonite literature. For a time, Frederick even took on the job of keeping the books for the Somerset Abode of Love. But gradually he began to sense that his family was being torn apart: he and Arnold on one side, and Rebecca and Dora on the other. And by the time he realised, it was too late. He had been replaced in his wife's and daughter's affections by the Reverend Pigott.

Frederick argued. He threatened. He even pleaded, as much as a Victorian industrialist could bring himself to plead. It was no good. Rebecca and Dora were leaving him to go where the Reverend Pigott led. Soon whispers reached Frederick's ears that his wife was having an affair with Pigott. Was it any wonder that in 1905 Frederick would be one of the directors to vote Charles Stokes Read off the board of the Vis Vitae Bread Company?

* * *

It was late spring in 1984. My sister had driven down from London to Dorset to stay with Hope Walpole and Lucy Bertram, two elderly sisters who, as children, had spent part of each year in the Abode of

Love. Their father had contributed £1,000 to the building of the Ark of the Covenant in London and the whole family had regularly been invited down to stay during the school holidays. They had soon made friends with our mother. Now in their 70s, they were only too happy to talk about the old days, even into a tape recorder.

'Belovèd used to have his services in what was called Eden . . . his sermons were wonderful,' said Hope, the elder of the two.

'Were they wonderful because of the way he told them or because of the content?' asked Ann.

'Both,' the sisters chorused.

'They were quite uplifting,' Hope continued. 'Well, as we came out – we'd all come out, sort of in procession – he would be standing at the door to sort of welcome everybody. As we went by, he would sometimes say something, or just smile, and just occasionally he would step forward and kiss us. That was a great honour, of course.'

'Did he kiss the men and the women?' Ann asked.

'I didn't see him doing it to any of the grown-ups,' answered Hope.

The two sisters talked about the wonderful holidays they enjoyed, so far from the smoke and dirt of London: the wonderful food, the frequent picnics – which our mother loathed – learning to dance, the plays the 'young ones' put on, the tennis parties. Hope recounted how one day she had smashed a window when a tennis shot went awry. 'Oh, you've no idea.' She giggled at the memory. 'All the elderly people came along to see the damage I had done.'

'What about Dora Beddow?' Ann asked.

'She used to play the organ,' recounted Hope. She and another young woman, one of Charles Read's daughters, also typed up the sermons, which were then reproduced and distributed to each follower, both in the Agapemone and in its scattered pockets across England, Norway and even North America. As the community aged, Dora took over the buying of food, driving into Bridgwater three times a week to purchase supplies.

'Did grandfather have an affair with her?' Ann suggested.

'There was something,' admitted Lucy. She recounted how one day she had asked Lavita, then a teenager, why Belovèd went to Dora's room every afternoon. Belovèd would have then been in his early 70s and Dora some 30 years younger. 'I'll tell you when you're older,' Lavita had replied loftily. The question was never satisfactorily answered.

'Was he an attractive man?' Ann asked.

'Yes, I suppose he was,' replied Hope. 'He had a very nice, gentle manner. Yes, I would say he was a very lovable person.'

But love wasn't everything, as it never is. Eventually, long after my grandfather's death, Dora would leave the community, disillusioned. 'What fools we have been,' she told my paternal grandmother and her sister, Great Aunt Tup. Dora was 74 when she died in Minehead Nursing Home.

16

☙

The Bequest

Jessie Fysh died.

Entry in the Agapemone diary
for Thursday, 15 October 1953

☙ I had never met Jessie Fysh. Yet the moment news of her death reached home, my mother and two uncles were talking about how she had left them between £10,000 and £11,000 in trust, whatever 'in trust' meant.

I was nearly always on my own when I had a weekend home from boarding school by this stage. But being the lone child in a house of elderly people had its advantages. I went almost unnoticed, something I soon learned to exploit. I found if I looked as though I was reading, everyone assumed I wasn't listening either. I did a lot of hanging about in tall wing chairs and horsehair sofas, open book in hand, in those days.

I soon learned that 92-year-old Jessie had once lived in the Agapemone but had gone to live with her sister in Weston-super-Mare, the seaside town in north Somerset. But she had never forgotten her happy days in my grandfather's community and left his children what seemed an enormous sum of money to my cash-strapped mother and uncles. Such a legacy, my mother and Uncle David argued, would surely ease their money problems, even after paying their brother's current debts and then dividing the remainder between the three of them.

But as with everything concerning money when it came to our family, there was a catch – Jessie's will had stipulated the money must be used for the religious purposes of the Church of the Ark of the Covenant in Clapton, north London. (I learned about this while staring vacantly at my book as I strained to keep track of yet another muttered conversation.) 'But a service hasn't been held there since just before you were born,' Mummy said to my uncle. 'Toto told me.'

'And that's damn near 50 years,' replied Uncle David. 'It's no good. I'll just have to make an appointment for us to see the solicitor to sort this out.'

'And spend more money,' countered Mummy.

'I don't see any alternative,' he replied.

The front door shut behind them. I heard the gravel scrunching beneath their feet as they made their way down the drive to the Lamb Inn for their pre-luncheon drink. I closed my book and eased myself off the leather sofa in the hall, where I had been lounging. It was time to find out more about this strange Ark of the Covenant.

The study was deserted, as I knew it would be between midday and one o'clock. The oval table, at which my grandmother, mother and uncles would lunch, was already laid with the ornate King's pattern silver that had once belonged to my father's family but which for many years had been used exclusively in Belovèd's End. Ellen would be having her own dinner in the kitchen parlour and would not return until just before ten to one, when she would bring Granny downstairs and guide her to her seat at the head of the table.

A fire crackled in the grate and Gay lay at full stretch on the hearth rug as I carefully picked my way between her long legs until I was close up to the small framed photograph of an ornate church which hung to one side of the fireplace.

Over lunch that day, I considered each of my fellow diners, wondering whom I could ask about the Ark of the Covenant. I had already discounted Waa, who had told me she had never visited it. Surely Violet Morris, who was an architect, would know. Besides, I loved visiting these two old ladies in their large East Gate home, with its bright, airy rooms and walled garden. I would spend an entire afternoon dusting all six drawers of Violet's egg collection. Other times, I would visit Olive in her carpentry studio just off the kitchens, where she would wield her chisels, planes, augers and carpenter's square, her hands moving with astonishing dexterity, despite her arthritic fingers.

Their sitting room was in darkness when I was ushered in later that afternoon. Tea had long finished and the two old ladies were waiting by their television for the news, which they would listen to at such a volume I could hear it from the road beyond their garden. I would have to ask my questions quickly before I was drowned out by the newsreader.

'What brings you here, miss?' bellowed Olive from her comfortable armchair.

'I've come to say goodbye,' I enunciated.

'And collect your usual?' she queried, with a knowing grin.

'Um-hm,' I acknowledged. The half-crowns which all the old ladies gave me whenever I returned to school made up most of my school pocket money. 'And I wanted to know something about the Ark of the Covenant.'

'Speak up, child.' Olive fumbled for her ear trumpet.

'SHE WANTS TO KNOW ABOUT THE ARK,' Violet shouted.

'Ah, poor Jessie! Never did have much sense, that one,' her sister retorted. 'They will soon go through her money, if they get their hands on it. Mark my words.'

Could she be talking about my mother and uncles, I wondered. And then I realised she must be when her sister shushed her with a warning glance in my direction.

'You've come to the right person, Kitty,' said Violet. 'My father and brother designed it. And I helped them.' I stared at the quiet little grey mouse of a woman before me with increased respect. Designing houses was one thing – I knew she had just finished working on one in the village – but a church?

She told me how in the 1890s Dear Belovèd was drawing such crowds with his preaching that a proper church was needed. A plot of land on Rookwood Road, near Clapton Common, was bought by a group of 13 people, including my great-grandfather Charles Stokes Read and Violet's father, who was a well-known architect and the county surveyor of roads and bridges for Berkshire.

Violet said she and her father and her brother Frank had put together a design which included a simple hall with a single-span, high-pitched roof, a semi-octagonal chancel, and a tower and spire at the western end. The church also contained several offices and meeting rooms below ground. 'It cost £15,000. That was a lot of money in those days,' she said. 'And the congregation raised all the money. Toto's father even paid for the hymn books.'

But Violet was most proud of the artwork, such as the statues, mosaics and, above all, those astonishing windows. 'What a time my father and brother had persuading Mr Crane to do the designs,' she recalled. 'It was his first attempt at stained-glass windows.'

'I carved the pulpit,' interrupted Olive, who had been following the conversation by waving the large end of her ear trumpet from one of us to the other.

'And what a day it was, when it opened,' Violet went on. 'Rookwood Road was jammed from one end to the other. People came from miles to see it.' Her face softened, 'Your grandfather preached the most wonderful sermon that day.'

'Why isn't it used now?' I asked.

'Because your mother and her brothers—' Olive burst out.

'Now, dear,' Violet interrupted. The mantel clock began chiming.

'Spoilt, that's what they were,' Olive continued muttering.

I thought back to Granny May's caustic comments about Mummy and her brothers. She wasn't alone in her view, it seemed.

'Time for the news,' Violet announced loudly, switching on the television set.

I said goodbye and left, disturbed by Olive's criticism of my mother and uncles but grateful for my new-found knowledge – plus the two half-crowns the old ladies had not forgotten to give me.

* * *

It was nearly nine o'clock that same evening when Gay began to growl, a deep throaty sound that filled the study and brought my mother and uncle up from their chairs.

'What's up, Gay?' My mother crossed the room and stroked the tall, leggy animal. Gay was attempting to push aside the net curtains that hung across the French windows looking out over Eden's garden. Her rangy body was vibrating, the sound coming from deep within her.

'There's someone out there,' said Uncle David.

'Perhaps it's the village constable doing his rounds?'

My uncle shook his head. 'Gay knows him; she'd never growl at him. I'm going to call the police.' He left the room.

'Do you think someone is trying to tar and feather us, like they did my great-grandfather?' I asked.

My mother's eyes widened. 'I'd forgotten you knew about that,' she admitted after a long pause. 'But no, Kitty, I don't think there's any danger of that. It's probably just a couple of village louts coming home from the pub and deciding it would be a lark to come in here.' She paused again and then, with concern in her voice, said, 'But I'm glad, Kitty, you didn't go over to the Ledermans this evening.'

'They're away.' I had got so used to spending the evening with them that when I found out they had left for a trip to Germany while I was at school I had felt bereft. Now I was quite glad I hadn't been coming back across the lawn alone, even though Mr or Mrs Lederman always watched me safely home from their doorway.

Uncle David returned within minutes to say the village constable had answered the phone himself, 'So it couldn't have been him.' He went on to report that the policeman would take a walk round the estate immediately. 'And in the meantime,' he said, 'no one should go out.'

My mother and uncle drew the heavy curtains across the windows, something they rarely bothered with. I followed them as they checked each of the mansion's several outside doors to make sure they were locked and bolted.

'I'll bet you, Lavita, it was that article about Jessie's money in the paper,' remarked my uncle. 'Pat showed it to me, today.'

'You'd think reporters would have better things to write about,' my mother replied.

'Why are the newspapers writing about us?' I asked, puzzled.

My mother and uncle stopped and turned, staring at me in surprise, as though they had forgotten I was still around. 'Because they have nothing better to do,' my uncle said flatly.

'And you, Kit, should be in bed. It's back to school tomorrow.'

I heard later that Uncle Pat showed up soon after with a cage in which squawked half a dozen grey-speckled Pearl guinea fowl.

'They're the best guard dogs there are; far better than geese,' he explained.

And so they proved, shrieking a forewarning from their perch in the top of Granny's blue cedar if anyone even tried the handle of the community's locked entrance door.

* * *

I was usually too busy at school to think about home, especially as I now had my pony and a friend had recently sold me a couple of baby rabbits, which I kept in a building set aside for students' pets. But the jibes about Mummy and my uncles being spoilt began to haunt me; they also seemed to imply that Waa was one of the culprits and she was beyond reproach as far as my sisters and I were concerned.

'Waa, were Mummy and the uncles spoilt when they were children?' I burst out the evening I returned home for the Christmas holidays. I was already in bed and Waa had come to tuck me in and switch out the light. It was a little ritual that brought me comfort every night of my childhood.

'Why do you ask, Kitty?' Waa lowered herself onto the bed, as if she had all the time in the world.

'Granny May said they were, when I stayed with her that time and then so did—' I hesitated, not wanting to sneak on Olive, or Emily (being a sneak at school was the very worst of crimes, one I was determined not to commit).

Waa smiled and patted my hand. 'They were very special, Kitty. They were Belovèd's children.' She stared into the distance, as if recalling those halcyon days. 'Were they spoilt? I don't think so. Certainly no more than any child should be spoilt.' She thought for a moment. 'Perhaps if anyone did any spoiling it was Katie. Oh, how she loved them.'

'She sounds nice.'

'She was a wonderful woman.' Waa rose from the bed. 'Remember, Kitty, a lot was expected of the three of them because they were Belovèd's children.'

'More than Daddy, when he used to stay here?'

'Much, much more.'

'Did Mummy and the uncles get into trouble if they were naughty?' That was my definition of spoilt. 'Like when Uncle Pat rode his bicycle through the picnic.'

Waa laughed, reaching to the bedside light and plunging the room into darkness. 'Do you know, Kitty, I simply can't remember.'

* * *

Having a pony of my own had given me a freedom of movement I had previously only imagined. Where once I would have not even dared to venture beyond the community gates – unless it was to the corner shop, and then only when I could be sure it would be empty of customers – during the summer of 1953 I found I could roam at will. No longer did I retreat when I caught sight of a group of village children. From high up in the saddle I could ignore this imagined enemy or, at the most, grandly lift my horse whip in greeting as Pinto clip-clopped by. This meant I could indulge my interest in collecting birds' eggs. Over the years, I had located just about every nest on the estate, but riding Pinto, I could roam much further afield, as well as spot any nests from my lofty perch atop him. I wanted a collection to rival Violet's, being careful to obey her rule of only one egg from each nest unless I was sure it had already been abandoned.

I had so much freedom, I often didn't even bother to return home for lunch. Nobody appeared to worry and nobody asked me where I had been when I returned in the late afternoon. Sometimes I would beg the kitchen to make me sandwiches, but mostly I told no one where I was going, preferring to merely stop at the village shop and buy a bottle of Tizer and a Crunchie bar. And then one day Mrs Lederman asked me if I would like to go to the seaside with them the following morning.

'Don't forget to ask your mother's permission,' she reminded me.

I was in the back seat of their car, along with David and baby Ruth, heading down the road when Mrs Lederman called over her shoulder from the front seat, 'You did remember to tell your mother, didn't you, Kitty?'

My heart sank. 'Yes,' I lied, comforting myself that no one would notice my absence.

I was in seventh heaven that day, doing what most ordinary families did: picnicking, playing catch on the wide sandy beaches of Weston-super-Mare, helping lug Ruth, now a lusty one year old, up and down the steps from the car. David and I even had a swim in the cold, shallow water.

It was dark by the time the car's headlights picked out the stables at home, where the Ledermans had been given permission to park their car. In their glow, I saw two figures hurrying towards us. Mummy's face was streaked with tears; behind her loomed Uncle David. Mr Lederman rolled down the car window.

'Is Kitty with you?' Mummy said as she thrust her head inside the car.

'Yes, she is,' replied Mr Lederman. 'Is something wrong?'

'We were just about to call the police,' replied my mother.

Terrified I might be banned from seeing the Ledermans, I confessed that I had lied to Mrs Lederman when asked if I had been given permission to accompany them. It was a tricky few days, with the whole community apparently having an opinion on how I should be punished, but they were gentle mutterings and within days it had blown over.

'Just don't do it again,' said my mother.

Perhaps, I wondered as I reflected on the lack of retribution, it wasn't just my mother and uncles who were spoilt.

* * *

That summer I had hoped to stay at school and watch the coronation of Elizabeth II, the new Queen of England, on the television set rented for the purpose by one of the teachers; however, the historic event had been decreed a national holiday and only those children whose parents were abroad were allowed to remain at school. On returning home for this unexpected holiday, I found the Ledermans again away. Worse still, from my entirely self-centred point of view, Olive Morris wasn't well; she had shingles, and so instead of watching the ceremony on television as I had expected, Waa and I, plus Margaret, who was home from art college, listened to it on the radio in one of the attic bedrooms.

Perhaps because we had not been able to watch the coronation, or perhaps because she had decided that Ellen was no longer up to the task – the elderly KP was getting decidedly doddery – my grandmother asked Margaret and me to clean out her curio cabinet. If only, I thought, she had asked a couple of years earlier, when the task would have put me in seventh heaven. Now, it seemed more like just another chore.

But the two of us dusted and cleaned every single tiny ivory saucepan and wooden cow before starting on the bottom shelf and a collection of long, flat presentation boxes in maroon imitation leather.

'I could use this for repairing that corner of the stable wall,' I said as I lifted a solid silver bricklayer's trowel out of the first box.

Margaret removed the trowel from my hands. 'It's not for use, Kitty. It's a presentation trowel.'

'What does that mean?'

'It's made to commemorate something, usually a building.'

'What building?'

'It could be the East Gate.' She held it up at an angle to read the inscription on the blade: 'Easter Sunday, 1905, Isaiah 54:10–12.'

I took the trowel from her and read the inscription for myself.

'Why don't you look the verse up in a Bible?' she suggested.

'I know where there's one.' I ran from the room to return moments later with my school Bible. Flicking to the right page, I began to read:

> For the mountains shall depart, and the hills be removed; but my kindness shall not depart from thee, neither shall the covenant of my peace be removed, saith the Lord that have mercy on thee.
>
> O thou afflicted, tossed with tempest, and not comforted, behold, I will lay thy stones with fair colours, and lay thy foundations with sapphires.
>
> And I will make thy windows of agates, and thy gates of carbuncles, and all thy borders of pleasant stones.

I looked up. 'Phew, that's a mouthful. What do you suppose it means?'

'Somewhere to go to that's peaceful?' suggested Margaret. 'Like here.' The silence of the afternoon enveloped us like a blanket. It was certainly peaceful.

'But carbuncles?' I searched for the verse. 'Gates of them?'

Margaret's eyes sparkled. 'Sounds like something to do with sore feet, like Ellen's corns.'

I returned to my room and fetched my school dictionary. Carbuncles, I read, could be red precious stones, malignant growths or small pieces of coal. 'You were half-right.' I said. 'But gates of rubies? We'd be rich!'

A few weeks later, Violet confirmed our suspicions. She told me how the trowel had been presented to Belovèd to commemorate the completion of the East Gate House, where she and her sister now lived but which she had designed as a retirement home for her parents. Then she took me outside and showed me the inscription carved into the house's loggia.

But that was in the future. Back on that afternoon, we continued cleaning until all that was left was the collection of delicate porcelain mugs that sat on the bottom shelf of the glass-fronted area of the cupboard. We had been instructed to take them to Granny's bathroom and wash them gently in her basin, using the rainwater tap.

'Margaret, why does this say Glory on it?' I asked as I deciphered the ornate Gothic letters painted on one side. I picked up a second mug. 'This one has the word Power on it.' Then a third. 'And this one says Life.'

'They're christening mugs.'

I looked at them again. 'That doesn't make sense. Glory, Power and Life aren't names. That's what you say in church, sort of.'

My sister stared at me. 'You mean you don't know that Uncle David's real name is Glory? And that Uncle Pat is Power. And Life – Lavita – is Mummy. *La vita* is Italian for 'the life', I think.'

'But they're not their *names*,' I protested, 'are they?' I searched my sister's face for that telltale sign she was teasing – the sparkle of glee in those huge dark brown eyes that always gave her away.

'I promise I'm telling the truth, Kitty.' She carefully laid the washed mugs back on the tray. 'Cross my heart and hope to die.' And then she grinned and I was plunged into doubt.

'I'm going to ask Waa.'

'Ask away – but not until we've finished.'

Waa confirmed that yes, those were their proper names and yes, she supposed I might think they were peculiar.

Peculiar! There was that word again. Could my mother's and uncles' weird names be one of what seemed a growing number of reasons why our family was thought 'peculiar'?

Glory, Power and Life! David, Patrick and Lavita! In the early entries of the Agapemone diary, Belovèd's children are always referred to by the extraordinary names they were given at their christenings. It is only in later years that they are referred to as David, Patrick – more often Panion – and Lavita. But why? I suspect that, as they became more aware of their situation and mixed with other children, such as my father's family of five boys, these three luckless members of the Holy Family were allowed to use more normal names.

17

Heady Times

Reverend Pigott embraced Brother Prince's religious philosophy with enthusiasm. Within months of that disastrous Irish venture in 1887, he and his wife Catherine had journeyed to Spaxton, where they had been warmly received by the now aging Prince. What a contrast the comfort and elegance of the closed community must have seemed after the poverty of the mission my grandfather had just abandoned. And, in turn, what a relief the arrival of such a charismatic young clergyman – he was barely 35 – must have been to Prince, by then in his late 70s. In addition, despite Prince's assertion that his followers would not die, time had moved on and the number of coffins being carried to burial on a nearby Somerset farm were steadily increasing.

In a letter to his north London flock, Prince recommended Reverend Pigott as pastor. Once again, my grandfather threw himself into his work, preaching spiritual ecstasy and conducting 'Nights of Prayer', so much so that each hall began to be filled to capacity. Many of these converts were of the rich merchant class and their families, while others were intelligent but under-challenged youngish women who, for one reason or another, had not married.

Once again, local newspapers began to sit up and take notice of the Agapemonites. The *Berkshire Chronicle* published an article about local 'recruiting missions' being carried out by James Ker, father of the old lady I knew as Toto. Another 'missionary' was William Fox, whose daughter, Louisa, would establish the diary that would record both the significant and obscure happenings of the Somerset Abode of Love for the next 70 years. Architect Joseph Morris, a former Quaker, and his family of gifted and eccentric children, opened their Berkshire home to services. George Kemp of Kemp Biscuits donated funds, and a lawyer from North Wales, who had also been drummed out of the Salvation Army, was appointed part-time pastor to the growing number of Agapemonites in that area. A convert journeyed to Norway and Sweden and began proselytising. Reverend Pigott soon followed and, according to the *British Weekly*, 'the doctrines spread, especially among the well-to-do people'.

It was a heady time for my grandfather. He was in his element, answerable only to an increasingly senile old man, far away in Somerset – no nervous bishops or overbearing priests, just an adoring flock, who hung on his every word. And for his ever-increasing numbers of middle-class followers, life had suddenly become more meaningful. There was also that frisson of excitement sparked by their leader's daring belief that they, his followers, were being gathered together to await a momentous event. And for some, a journey down to the Somerset headquarters and the Abode of Love was a chance to witness this paradise in action: life in a beautiful part of the country with no material worries; a place where they could literally leave the world behind. For those who had joined from the working classes, the Agapemone offered security from the dreaded workhouse.

The Reverend Pigott's arrival on the scene gave the movement the boost it needed to survive. And not just survive but soar to unimaginable heights, as this new pastor embraced the sect's beliefs.

By 1892, it had become clear that those followers in the London area needed a place of worship they could call their own.

On 29 September 1892, a group of followers, led by my grandfather, purchased a plot of land on Rookwood Road in Clapton, north London, for £1,200. The group included my stockbroker great-grandfather Charles Stokes Read, an architect, plus a chartered accountant, civil engineer, tax collector, master baker, and Prince's daughter Eva, by his spiritual bride. Among the conditions of purchase drawn up in copperplate writing on enormous sheets of parchment was the stipulation – which was surely insisted on by my grandfather – that neither the land nor any buildings erected on it could ever be used by the Church of England or the Salvation Army.

A couple of months after the land was bought, the group decided to build a church, and in the document, dated 30 December 1892, in which they drew up their intentions, they stated the building was

> . . . to be used by and for all the purposes of the body of people which acknowledging the doctrine of the Trinity in Unity as expressed in the creed commonly called the Apostles Creed worship the Lord Jesus Christ in his New Name as the Son of Man and believe in the Holy Ghost as having fulfilled the Gospel in 'Brother Prince' and as being the Covenant Head of the Dispensation of Judgment, introduced by Brother Prince whose teaching is contained in his writings 'The Man Christ Jesus' and 'The Counsel of God in Judgment'.

No expense was to be spared. Architect Joseph Morris and his son, Francis, designed a high Victorian 'muscular Gothic' place of worship with a single-span pitched roof, a semi-octagonal chancel and a western tower topped by a spire visible for miles. Member of the Royal Academy and fashionable sculptor Arthur G. Walker created the stone and bronze sculptures depicting strange winged creatures from the Book of Revelations set at the foot of the spire and the base of the tower. A builder known for his work in the art nouveau style also joined the project and hired accomplished woodworkers to build the pews with their intricately carved ends.

Overseeing this extravagant scheme, which drew daily crowds of curious passers-by, was a local justice of the peace, who had been hired 'by the special request of Mr Pigott'. The Ark of the Covenant took three years to complete. Its £15,000 cost was funded entirely by the faithful.

And at last the day dawned when this strange church was to be formally opened. It was Whit Sunday 1896. Within the space of no more than half an hour, each of the four hundred seats had been taken, with everyone dressed in their best and squeezed into the long rows of pews. Although the vast majority were local believers and those who had made the journey from Somerset, there were representatives of every known Agapemonite cell, from Sweden, Norway, Germany, America and even India. Curious members of the press and public were allocated the few seats left vacant.

Everything must have seemed possible in those heady months following the dedication of the Ark of the Covenant. Brother Prince returned to Somerset, content in the knowledge that the movement he had created was in such safe hands. Now in his late 80s, he was growing tired. He no longer recruited followers, but surrounded himself with a handful of sycophantic and aging followers. He no longer preached but spent the day reclining on a chaise longue, being administered to by his now elderly spiritual wife and adult daughter. Gone was his vehemence about the evils of alcohol. 'Perfectionism' reigned. The Agapemone cellar was kept stocked with fine wines, which he enjoyed with luncheon and dinner. And in a somewhat pragmatic Christian spirit, Prince insisted that the poor of the village continued to be looked after.

Only when religious necessity arose did Prince summon his London pastor and Smyth-Pigott's delightful wife down to Somerset and away from the young pastor's important work in the capital.

By 1899, the nineteenth century – and Prince's life – was drawing to a close. One day, the 88-year-old Prince visibly began to fade. Worried, Douglas Hamilton sent word to the Reverend Smyth-Pigott in London. My grandfather hurried to Somerset, just in time for his dying leader to see him and, legend has it, call out 'Belovèd' before he expired.

Prince's followers were confused, appalled and frightened at his death. When others had died it had been easy to dismiss their parting as a failure on their part, but Brother Prince? Surely not. It took all my grandfather's considerable skill to soothe the confused faithful and at the same time get the old man laid to rest in the garden of the Somerset Abode of Love in what I was to know as Katie's Corner.

18

🔖

The Second Coming

🔖 Three years later, the ornate church on Rookwood Road had achieved a kind of curiosity value. In the pews would be seated the occasional middle-class matron, who would comment on the sermons or the order of service – like that of the Anglican matins 'but strangely different'. Some who entered its portals might tut-tut, 'Those hymns!' While others might comment on their fellow churchgoers, 'who for all the world look just like us, my dear!'

The doors of this strange church would then be closed to the public without warning, sometimes for weeks at a time. That was when the rumours began.

Newspaper reporters wrote about the various theories being put forward by neighbours of this Ark of the Covenant. One was that the now-secret services had something to do with the Mysteries of Eleusis of the Ancient Greeks and involved symbolic sacrifices that were a foreshadowing of the Christian sacrament of the Eucharist. A report that Smyth-Pigott had once been a common sailor was quickly seized on as proof that these Mysteries of Eleusis were somehow involved because it was well known that sailors in fear for their lives at sea asked each other if they had been initiated at Eleusis.

Another speculative report suggested that the secret services were to do with Sophocles. Hadn't the great philosopher said, 'Thrice blessed are they who behold these mystical rites, ere passing to Hades' realm. They alone have life there. For the rest all things below are evil.'

But just as suddenly, the church would reopen its doors to the public and it soon became clear there was still nothing particularly strange about the services: just singing hymns from an admittedly unusual hymn book and calls to salvation by the pastor and members of his congregation.

Strangers were welcomed. It became fun, almost daring, to attend the Sunday services, even though many left unimpressed by the long convoluted address by the pastor, even with his vivid imagery. But he was attractive and so others stayed, many of them single women in their 30s, who, facing the prospect of lifelong spinsterhood and all its strictures, answered my grandfather's siren call of the imminent arrival of the Second Coming.

During one of the unannounced closures of the church in early August 1902, a newspaper reporter, no doubt desperate for a story in the dog days of summer, went to investigate. 'We – the world – is on the verge of a crisis,' warned the only church member the reporter could find who would speak to him. 'God alone knows. There is a terrible crisis at hand.' But the elderly gentleman would say no more and the reporter gave up and went back to his boss, editor of the *Hackney and Kingsland Gazette*. The story was spiked.

But not for long.

No one knows whether the reporter decided to continue delving into this strange sect or whether he received a tip-off that it might be in his interests to attend evensong on Sunday, 7 September 1902. My grandfather had turned 50 on 1 August.

When the reporter arrived, a little late, he found the church packed to overflowing and the congregation singing the first hymn. He squeezed into a back row next to a lady accompanying two children dressed in white. She smiled at the reporter's whispered apologies and offered to share her hymn book. Others seated in the row in front also turned and smiled at him. 'The interior of the ark is white stone beautifully carved, the seats are of a light oak colour, and beyond them, in a semicircular altar, reached by carpeted steps, was a throne, before which was placed a table of white marble,' read the reporter's account in the 10 September edition of the *Hackney and Kingsland Gazette*. It went on:

> Upon this throne was seated a tall emaciated man, with a sallow countenance, dark and glittering black eyes, thin black hair parted down the centre of a small head, but otherwise clean-shaven. He was dressed like a clergyman. Around him at the bottom of the dais were seated several men without any distinguishing vestments . . .
>
> It appeared to be a very well-dressed congregation, hardly any poorly-clothed people, such as you see in other churches, being present . . . Several times, for instance, one of the (presumably) members of the church turned and, with a smile, pointed out the place of the hymns in the hymn book . . .
>
> The singing was accompanied by the notes of a small organ. At its conclusion there was a deep silence, which lasted for quite half a minute, during which no movement was made. Then the dark young man sitting on the throne got up slowly and still more slowly walked round the table to the centre of the dais. There he stood for a time looking fixedly at the congregation facing him.
>
> Then speaking softly, almost musically, and with deliberation, he said: 'It is appointed unto man once to die and after this the judgment. Christ suffered for sin and it was promised that for them who waited for Him He would appear a second time with the salvation to man from death and

judgment. Brother Prince was sent before his Lord's face to prepare this way, to prepare the way for the Second Coming of Him who suffered for sin, to prepare the way for the restoration of all things. His testimony was true and the work of the Holy Ghost in him was perfect, and I who speak to you tonight, I am that Lord Jesus Christ who died and rose again and descended into heaven; I am that Lord Jesus come again in my own body to save those who come to me from death and judgment. Yes, I am He that liveth, and behold I am alive for ever more – the Lord from heaven and Life giving Spirit to those who know me and come to me. I am come again for the second time as the Bridegroom of the Church and the Judge of all men, for the Father has committed all judgment to me because I am the Son of Man. And you, each one of you, must be judged by me . . .'

The speaker again paused for several seconds, gazing abstractedly on his hearers. Then with a sudden re-enlightenment of his eyes and lifting of his hands he resumed: 'It is not up there – in heaven – where you will find your God, but in me who am united with the Father . . . Yet no man can come to me except the Father who sends me brings him for every man who really desires to know God will be taught by him and will come to me.'

The reporter was stunned. He re-read his notes. Yes, that's what the preacher had said: 'I am the Son of Man!' Later, the reporter would note:

For this startling denouement there was nothing to prepare the visitor . . . It was quite obvious that many others in the church were unprepared for the announcement upon whom the reiterated testimony to the claim produced in one or two cases a dramatic effect.

But not initially:

> The speaker moved his head slowly from side to side, and then slowly walked back to his throne, where he sat for a time with his head buried in his hands. After this there was a silence until a well-dressed woman got up in the centre of the congregation. 'Every word he has spoken,' she said, 'God has spoken. God is here. I see him on the altar.'
>
> An old grey-haired man got up and said, 'Behold that is Christ.'
>
> The speaker appeared to be quite calm.
>
> 'Behold that is God,' said another.
>
> 'The Desire of all nations,' said another.
>
> 'Behold I testify to the Lord God,' came from someone else . . .
>
> At last a man, who appeared to be a stranger sitting next to the Leader representative, fell down convulsively on to his knees, his eyes full of tears, and dragging his wife on to her knees with him, said, 'God, Annie, that is Jesus.'

It was not the only scene:

> The last testimony having been given, several of those present addressing themselves to the figure on the throne, cried aloud, 'Oh hail! Hail! Holy man!' after which the entire body of those present said, 'O hail thou King of Glory,' at the conclusion of which the figure on the throne rose up and, in an ecstatic voice, said, 'Peace! Peace be with you.'

It was to be anything but.

'THE ARK STORMED. RIOTOUS CROWDS THREATEN THE AGAPEMONITES' screamed the *Morning Leader* of 9 September 1902:

Some two hundred of the five or six thousand people who assembled on Clapton Common yesterday morning [8 September] got into the Agapemone or Abode of Love [*sic*] and heard the Revd J.H. Smyth-Pigott declare himself to be the Messiah on his Second Coming.

The police arrangements to cope with the crowd were quite inadequate, and the long queue that had been formed was broken up by a sudden and ugly rush, in which several women were bruised. The chapel was carried by assault, and dozens clambered over the railings after the gates were shut. Both on arrival and departure Mr Pigott was hissed and groaned at, but attempts to strike him were warded off by police . . . There were at least 3000 outside when the faithful began to arrive . . . the women were the most vehement . . . the men usually chaffed the congregation, fitting Biblical names to them with some appositeness and asking when the miracles were going to begin . . . Mr Pigott stepped out [of his coach] with a lady . . . Vigorous hissing and hootings greeted him. His response was to remove his hat and stare at the people with a weird and inscrutable smile upon his lips . . . After Mr Pigott had entered the building . . . about twenty men of the Salvation Army marched to the front of the church singing lustily, 'We shall know him'. 'Halt,' said the captain, who then stepped forward and addressed the people. 'Be it known unto you,' he said, 'that there is no other way of forgiving sins save through the Lord Jesus Christ . . .' As they marched away again, the significance of this dramatic little interlude was not lost . . . There was an ominous swaying and a sudden and irresistible forward move . . . they hammered on the door in a very noisy manner . . . about two hundred of those who had got into the grounds were admitted . . . when the strange service was over, the crowd rushed out pell-mell . . . [Mr Pigott] came out shortly, still smiling and calm and was seen into his brougham by police . . . a mounted policeman galloped a lane through the crowd . . . thousands of people [ran] over the common after the carriage, yelling and hissing and uttering threats . . .

Half a century later, the coachman who made that dash to carry my grandfather to safety recounted the events of that day to a *Daily Express* reporter. The story was published on 16 December 1955. 'Blimey, what a to-do!' recalled Alfred Rawlings, then 82:

Old Smyth-Pigott had said he was the Lord and word, of course, spread like lightning. I mean to say, you're asking for trouble if you go around saying things like that. Well of course, there were hundreds of people waiting for us. They were shouting and roaring. I whipped the coach round smartly and headed for home. The mob chased us right across Clapton Common shouting 'hypocrite' and things like that – a lot worse. We went to Smyth-Pigott's house, he and the missus nipped in smartly . . .

On 15 September 1902, the *Hackney and Kingsland Gazette* reported:

The sensation caused by the blasphemous antics of the Reverend J.H. Smyth-Pigott culminated yesterday in one of the most disgraceful scenes that have ever desecrated an English Sabbath . . . the roadway was completely blocked and rendered impassable . . . fresh reinforcements of police came on the scene, but they were powerless . . . [inside the church, Mr Pigott's preaching] was evidently too much for the unconverted portion of the audience, who vented their disapproval with cries of 'Humbug,' 'Nonsense,' 'Liar' . . .

Two days later, the same newspaper published the following:

Reverend J.H.S. Pigott left Clapton on Monday for the Abode of Love at Spaxton . . . news that he was to arrive at Bridgwater en route for Spaxton seems to have caused great excitement . . . a crowd of several hundred proceeded to the railway station. Directly the train came in all eyes scanned the carriages and presently a clergyman was seen to emerge . . . he was a short man and wore a straw hat . . . instantly there was a big rush . . . the clergyman was considerably hustled by the crowd and there were several ugly rushes . . . [the stationmaster] assured the crowd that this was not Mr Pigott, but the crowd was incredulous and the carriage drove away amid much booing and hooting.

And on 22 September 1902:

As generally anticipated, no services were held at the 'Ark of the Covenant' . . . the Reverend Mr Pigott will avoid all appearances in public until the popular resentment caused by his blasphemous claim to be the Messiah has somewhat abated . . . evidence of the state of excitability into which the people of north London have been thrown by Mr Smyth-Pigott's claim to Divinity was afforded Friday night by an extraordinary scene at Dalston Junction.

Between seven and eight o'clock a carriage was drawn up to the north London station, and to an inquiry as to who he was waiting for the coachman jokingly replied, 'Mr Smyth-Pigott.' As if by magic the rumour spread that the leader of the Agapemonites was on the station, and in an incredibly short space of time a crowd of people in a state of angry excitement had gathered. Before long, the streets in the immediate neighbourhood were quite impassable to vehicular traffic . . . [railway officials] closed the station . . . a strong body of constables were quickly marched to the scene . . . [but] as train after train deposited its passengers the crowd, instead of being decreased, swelled to greater proportions . . . the scene was of the wildest description . . . it was late in the evening before it was deemed advisable to open the station gates to other passengers.

Was my grandfather losing his nerve? Was he regretting his extraordinary claim? Certainly, he cancelled all services at his Ark of the Covenant until further notice. But even that did not stop what the *Hackney and Kingsland Gazette* dubbed 'the idle and the curious' from hanging around outside the church hoping for more excitement. 'Sunday lecturers' made their appearance, hoping to capitalise on the crowds, but without success. Their strange beliefs were listened to politely and then ignored, as the crowd dispersed.

Other pretenders to divinity appeared. The *Hackney and Kingsland Gazette* reported: 'A French rival to Mr. Pigott has come forward.' He was apparently found 'wearing a long robe haranguing a large crowd in the main street at Fontenay near Paris'. The police carted him off to a lunatic asylum. In Kentish Town, London, a shoeblack argued that he too was the reincarnation of the Messiah and anyone rejecting his claim would be rejected by God.

But the reporter who had broken the story was not to be diverted. He stationed himself outside the nearby lodgings of the 'Messiah' and was just in time to see 'a gentleman whose name is not unknown in Debrett [*sic*] and who at one time had a seat in the House of Commons' arrive and be admitted.

When he re-emerged about an hour later, the gentleman related how he had spoken with a Mr Douglas Hamilton, secretary to Mr Pigott. The secretary had explained, he said, that it wasn't surprising that Christ had come in the body of Mr Pigott because Christ had changed his appearance many times after the crucifixion – as a gardener when he appeared to Mary Magdalene, as a stranger to two of his disciples on the road to Emmaus. The unnamed former Member of Parliament said he had countered that the true identity of

Christ had been confirmed when he had shown to St Thomas the marks of the nails in his hands and feet. Hamilton, he reported, had repeated that Christ had appeared in many different characters.

The letters pages of area newspapers were overwhelmed. Heading a column's worth on 26 September 1902 is – along with comments on 'the state of the roads' and 'the wicked education bill' – 'the Clapton "messiah"'.

'. . . Pity him,' wrote D.W. Miller, 'I do not believe him to be a hypocrite, but a man of great religious feeling, though sadly deluded . . . Had Mr Pigott developed his reason a little more he would not have been victim of his absurd delusion.' And he wasn't the only one.

By October, my grandfather had shaken off the dust of disbelieving London and repaired to his Abode of Love in Somerset, where he was greeted with a mixture of awe, delight and supplication. It was left to loyal Douglas Hamilton to deal with this latest skirmish with Church authorities. A Reverend Browne of Crouch End had written asking to publicly debate Mr Pigott on his Messianic claims. 'We have nothing to debate,' replied Hamilton.

Moreover, he continued, future correspondence would not be forthcoming unless the Messiah was approached 'in the attitude of supplication'. The Reverend J.H. Smyth-Pigott had 'ceased to be'.

19

A Secret Revealed

1954 – the Agapemone diary records no entries for the year I learned about my grandfather's stupendous blasphemy. Was that a coincidence? Back then, had I known, I would have been convinced my reaction to my new-found knowledge had upset those I lived with to such an extent that no one that year even gave a thought to the diary that had recorded the community's momentous and trivial happenings for half a century. Now, I believe it was indeed merely chance.

It was term time and I had lined up with the rest of the student body for the weekly distribution of sweets: any confectionery brought to school at the start of each term was confiscated and then doled out every Saturday morning, when it could be supplemented by sweets bought by the school and resold to us. How we looked forward to Saturdays.

I remember so well the way the sun streamed through the huge glass cupola above the grand staircase that morning, adding warmth to the busy hum of 90 schoolgirls. At last, it was my turn and I collected my ration of the Belgian chocolates I had brought for the summer term – a gift from one of the old ladies – adding to them five Liquorice Allsorts and two Bulls Eye mints.

Belgian chocolates were hardly the usual confection brought in by pupils. But then neither was the armful of damask tablecloths or the eight-piece set of solid silver cutlery in its own leather roll that I had been sent to school with in my first term. Most parents just provided the requisite knife, fork and spoon, plus two sheets of bed linen.

I enjoyed the rush of exquisite taste as I left the queue. 'Kitty!' I heard someone call out.

'Yup,' I shouted over my shoulder. Stuffing the rest of the chocolates in the paper bag they had been distributed in, I waited impatiently for a friend, whose identity I have forgotten, to catch up. I was anxious to get Pinto and ride down to the beach a mile or so away, where we would gallop into the sea and I would feel his muscles rippling beneath me as he began to swim.

'Did you know,' my friend said as she fell into step beside me, 'your grandfather said he was Jesus?'

I had no idea what she was talking about. 'Huh?'

'Your grandfather, Smyth-Pig . . . pig . . . oh, whatever his name was, said he was Jesus.'

'Don't be stupid.'

'I'm not,' she persisted. 'I heard my aunt and Mummy talking about the Aga . . . Agap . . . your home, anyway, when they drove me to school. And they said your grandfather said he was Jesus.'

'Well, they're wrong,' I retorted. I turned away, fished another sweet out of my pocket and began to head downstairs. 'Nobody goes around saying they're Jesus!'

'You ask Miss Burridge,' she shouted after me.

I made my way out of the main school building and down the drive to the stables, snatched my pony's halter from its hook in the tack room and strode out to the park to call him. How dare she talk such nonsense? And she calls herself a friend!

But when I got to the park I realised I had come without a carrot – I would have to entice Pinto with my one remaining sweet. As I toiled after my pony under an increasingly hot sun, I began to work myself up into a state of righteous indignation over my friend's words. But they would not go away, stretching instead like a banner across my mind. I had to get to the bottom of this. To my pony's surprise, I abandoned trying to catch him and returned to the school, where I tracked down the headmistress, Miss Lilian Burridge, who was chatting with her sister Miss Mary, the school matron, outside the little ones' dormitory.

'Is something wrong, Kitty?' asked Miss Mary, seeing my expression.

Her kindly-put question crystallised my years of unanswered confusion about my family into something close to panic. Suddenly, I couldn't speak.

Once we were seated in the alcove of her bedroom, I began. 'Someone told me my grandfather claimed he was Jesus.'

The two sisters' expressions were far too noncommittal.

'It's not true,' I whispered, 'is it?'

'He didn't exactly say he was Jesus, dear,' said Miss Lilian.

Relief began to flood through me.

'It was more that he was the Messiah. The Second Coming,' she went on, with a glance at her sister, who nodded in confirmation.

I watched their lips move and heard not a word. Surely, it couldn't be true! And yet . . . they would not lie to me; not as they were so religious, running their little school according to their Christian beliefs. Eventually, Miss Lilian left the room, reappearing several minutes later with the stuttering Reverend Skrine.

His mollifying explanation made no difference. I didn't even hear what he said, I was so consumed by the thought that my grandfather didn't even look like Jesus. No long hair. No blue eyes. No robes.

It seemed like hours – but could have been seconds – before the vicar excused himself and Miss Mary asked if I would like to go home for the rest of the weekend.

'Are you expelling me?'

She smiled. 'Why would I do that, Kitty? We thought a weekend home would give you a chance to talk the whole thing over with your family. To ask questions.'

And be told answers!

By the time Mummy arrived in a taxi to fetch me – promptly, for once – I was stony-faced. The drive home took place in silence. I wasn't saying anything in front of strangers; I knew my mother wouldn't. When we reached home and Waa came out to greet me, I pushed past her, ran up to my room and locked myself in.

Flinging myself onto my bed, I glared up at the ceiling. All those hours in the school chapel. All those Sunday mornings in church. Praying to Jesus. The scripture lessons about Jesus. The little talks from Miss Mary about Jesus. And all the time . . .

'Kitty?' Mummy's voice came from beyond the door. I watched the door handle turn. 'Come on, Kitty, open this door!'

Perhaps I would refuse to go back to school. But Pinto was at school. Maybe I would become a nun. No, not a nun – fancy praying, 'Our Grandfather, who art in heaven!'

Then it was Uncle David – Uncle Glory! 'Kitty, listen to your mother.'

'Go away!' I screamed. It had the desired effect. The door handle stopped turning and the footsteps receded. No wonder Ann had been so keen to leave. Her boyfriend had been right, our family truly was 'peculiar'.

I must have fallen asleep for the next thing I remembered was it being dusk. It took me a few seconds to work out where I was. And why. So, this was no nightmare from which I would awake. I felt my heart sink. Perhaps I was about to have a heart attack and they would find me dead in bed. Then they would be sorry.

My stomach rumbled in the silence. I realised I was starving. How could such a prosaic need as food make itself felt when my life had been devastated? I glanced at my watch – eight o'clock. Everyone would be in bed except Mummy and Uncle David, and they would be at the pub or in Granny's drawing room at the other end of the house. Another rumble. I would have to creep down to the kitchens and find something – anything – to eat. But before I even made it out of bed, someone knocked on my bedroom door.

'Kitty!' It was Waa. 'I've brought you some toast and tea. Shall I leave it out here?'

'Yes,' I said shortly. 'No.' I padded to the door and unlocked it. Waa was in her dressing gown, her white hair unpinned and straggling down her back. She carried a tray, which she set on my bedside table. Tea, a whole mound of hot buttered toast and an egg under its own little cosy.

'Oh, Waa,' I cried, my tears beginning to flow.

'I know.' She pulled me to her.

'Why wasn't I told?'

'Mummy so hates to see any of you upset. She loves you all very much.'

'Do Ann and Margaret know?'

'Yes, they know. I think we all thought they might tell you. Sometimes things are easier coming from people your own age.'

Anger, this time at my sisters, rose like bile. 'Well, they didn't.' My voice began to rise. 'Why didn't they, Waa?'

'They probably didn't want to think about it either.'

'Do you believe my grandfather was Jesus?'

She didn't answer immediately and, feeling betrayed, I started to pull free from her encircling arms. 'But it wasn't how it was, Kitty,' she went on. 'Your dear grandfather never said he was Jesus – Jesus died on the cross – he said he was the Son of Man, come again to help the world. And, Kitty, if the world had listened, maybe those terrible wars would never have happened and my brothers would never have been killed.'

She poured the tea and pointed to the egg and pile of toast. 'Eat up, Kitty. It'll help,' she encouraged. 'Your grandfather was a wonderful man, who acted according to his lights.'

'He was a blasphemer! He was a false prophet!' I shouted, cracking the egg so violently, the yolk streamed down the side of the shell. I scooped it up with my finger.

She looked at me as I sat in bed, hugging my knees, with a tear-streaked face and fingers covered in egg yolk. 'The world called him that. But he made us all feel special and he so wanted the world to be a better place. And he entrusted me, Kitty – young Margaret Davis from Wiltshire – with his children. And now you and your sisters are my family, too, and I wouldn't have had it any other way. Not for all the tea in China.'

I should have tossed and turned that night and awoken the next morning with rings of exhaustion under my eyes, but I hardly remembered my head hitting the pillow after Waa left. It was in the daylight that the nightmare returned. One moment I convinced myself none of it was true; the next, I worried about what was I going to say to people; and the next, who else knew? Did the Ledermans know? No wonder the village children laughed at me. Waves of embarrassment flooded through me at the thought of everyone knowing but me. Would my friends shun me, like in the Bible? I shouldn't have had to discover the truth about my grandfather from a school friend. But, most of all, I was angry with this grandfather I had never known but who had coloured my entire life. Who had spoiled everything – from beyond the grave!

Eventually, I washed and dressed and made my way along the passage, through the baize door to Granny's End and down the dark stairs to her drawing room. People are right when they say they see things in a different light: nothing had actually changed – around me old ladies moved like old snails, nodding and smiling as I squeezed past; the same bucket sat under the same leak, on the bottom step of the stairs leading to Jericho; the same gloomy Victorian engravings hung on the wall, including one which had always terrified me, of a wolf about to attack a small child in her four-poster bed – yet it didn't look the same.

Halfway down Granny's stairs, I stopped to stare up into my grandfather's penetrating, sad eyes gazing down from his portrait. I longed to throw something at it. 'What are you doing, Kitty?' Mummy was watching me from the drawing-room doorway.

'Staring at Jesus,' I replied.

She sighed. 'This isn't worthy of you.' She opened the door wider. 'Ethel has made some coffee. Real coffee, not instant,' she enticed.

'I don't like coffee,' I lied. 'I'm going to see Granny.'

'Granny isn't here. Uncle David has taken her out for the day.'

'So I won't ask her questions?'

'Yes,' replied my mother. 'She's an old lady, Kitty. She's blind and she has cancer.' She pushed the door wide for me. 'Come in here.'

The morning sun streamed in, setting the Crown Derby in the glass-fronted sideboard a-sparkle and making patterns of light on the oval dining table. Mummy sat opposite me. 'I can't really tell you much, Kitty, because it all happened before I was born.'

'All what happened?'

'He announced he was the Second Coming.'

'And people believed him.' My tone dripped with all the sarcasm I could muster.

'Many did,' my mother admitted. 'But many more didn't.'

After breakfast, I wandered outside and gazed longingly at the neat little house where my friends, the Ledermans, lived. I could see Trudel Lederman inside dusting. She looked up and, seeing me, waved. I waved back and forced a smile. No, I couldn't face explaining why I was home in the middle of term. I turned away.

At lunch, I tried to imagine the old ladies praying to, rather than with, my grandfather. Did they genuflect when they saw him, as my mother and uncle did when they went to Roman Catholic Mass? As soon as we'd finished eating, I hurried to the laundry.

Cissy peered up at me from the door of the little low cottage. 'Oh, it's you, Kitty. I thought you were at school,' she said. 'Never mind, I had hoped it might be the doctor. Lettit has had a fainting spell. Probably doing too much as usual. We're all getting old, I'm afraid, Kitty.' She thrust a coin into my jodhpur pocket. 'It's all we have on us at the moment, but perhaps it will buy you a little something. Everything's getting so expensive these days.'

I sought out Emily.

'Go about your business, young lady,' she raged, when I raised the subject. 'Or I'll take my stick to your back. You don't know what you're talking about.'

I went back to Waa.

'He acted according to his lights,' she said. 'It's all I can say, dear. It's all in the past and best forgotten.'

'But nobody does forget. They're always talking about him and how wonderful he was, yet you're all cross with me when I ask questions!' I wailed, close to tears.

She reached for me and, tall as I was – a good head and shoulders taller than her bent old figure – she clutched me to her. 'I know, Kit, I know. But you have to put it behind you. You're making everyone unhappy.'

My uncle and grandmother returned from their outing in the late afternoon. I had promised my mother not to talk to my grandmother, so I turned my burning anger and confusion on my uncle.

'Now perhaps you know what it was like for your mother, Uncle Pat and me,' he replied angrily to my questioning.

'I don't care what it was like for you; it's terrible for me!' I shouted. 'I hate my home. And I hate my family.'

Uncle David spat out his answer. 'You ungrateful wretch!' he cried. 'Try being in our shoes; then you'd know!'

Mummy had been sitting quietly in a corner chair. 'Perhaps now, Kitty,' she interrupted, 'you can understand why I sent you to boarding school. So you could have a life beyond this place.'

'I wish I could stay there and never come home,' I yelled as I ran from the room.

Over the next 24 hours, I nursed my confusion into a cold determination to find out all I could. I chose my time and victim carefully. Waa had returned to her ever-growing pile of my mending. Mummy and Uncle David were at the pub. The KP were at lunch.

'Did someone knock?' Toto called from her room.

'It's me. Kitty.'

She opened her door. 'What a lovely surprise! Come in, come in.' She took my arm and guided me to a chair, as if it was me who was going blind.

'I want to know about my grandfather,' I burst out.

'He left us a long time ago.' She shook her head sadly. 'We never dreamed he would leave us. Oh, it was such a terrible time. Especially for our Holy Family.'

I blinked. 'Holy Family?'

'Yes, dear, your grandfather, your grandmother, and your mother and uncles.'

What did that make me? And my sisters? It was becoming so bizarre, I didn't know whether to laugh or cry. But it was Toto who began to cry. A tear magnified into a huge bubble from behind her bottle-end glasses and then started down her cheek. She wiped at it with her lace hanky.

'It was all such a long time ago, Kitty. So much has happened since then, so much confusion and sadness.'

Watching her, I grew scared. Suddenly, I hadn't the heart to badger her. 'Please don't cry, Toto.'

I went back to my mother, who said again how it had all happened long before she was born. 'You can't imagine how hard I tried to leave this all behind me,' she said, as she sipped her third whisky of the evening. 'But remember, Kit, he was my father and I loved him very much.'

Eventually, Uncle David, in his quick-tempered way, told me to stop pestering the old people and my mother. 'You're becoming a spoilt brat,' he said. I didn't know what I was talking about. I was being so self-indulgent. I led a normal life, went to boarding school –

at great financial cost to my mother, he went on, as he departed for sea again – to my great relief. What more did I want? I wanted the truth about my grandfather's astounding declaration on Sunday evening, 7 September 1902.

* * *

As I watched the taxi, which had brought me back to school, wend its way down the drive, the waves of confusion which had surged through me when I had first learned of my grandfather's stupendous claims continued to ebb and flow, a bit like seasickness. I continued to struggle with my new knowledge for the rest of the term. The first thing to go was my embryo faith. I no longer even tried to pay attention to Reverend Skrine's sermons or the Misses Burridge's teachings about 'the Lord', and how one must never 'take His name in vain'. Well, my family had blown that, hadn't they?

Little did I know then that the kindly Burridges routinely shielded me and my younger cousins, who also attended St Hilda's, from the frequent newspaper stories about the Agapemone and its once-scandalous goings-on – yet another example of the kindness and loving atmosphere within that small and unfashionable school.

If my grandfather had said he was the Son of God come again – and been so obviously wrong – then perhaps Jesus hadn't been the Son of God either? I was perfectly ready to agree that the hero of the New Testament was a good man, but the Son of God? What God? I didn't doubt there was once a good man named Jesus, who righted wrongs and was crucified because he represented a threat to the state, but was he perhaps just one among many, including Muhammad and Buddha? Perhaps there was no God, just a force for good and a force for evil.

Much of my initial anger about my ignorance was directed towards my sisters, who had both now left home. But I reserved my deepest anger for my mother, my uncles and those I lived with. Surely, I should not have been left to find out from a school friend. As the term wound on, I promised myself that as my family hadn't been honest with me, I would have nothing to say to them.

When at last I returned home for the holidays, to my shame I was rude to Waa, curt with my mother and uncles, and merely polite to the old ladies. But I did shrink from behaving badly in my grandmother's presence, just as I shrank from confronting her about my grandfather's outrageous claim.

But I had to talk to someone.

One afternoon just before teatime, my curiosity got the better of me and despite my resolve not to speak to my family – and Toto was family as far as I was concerned – I plucked up my courage and tiptoed to her room on the top floor of the mansion. I knocked on her door. What if she started crying again? That thought almost sent me scuttling back down the steep stairs. But I was too late. 'Who's there?' The old lady peered out from behind her thick spectacles.

'It's me. Kitty.'

She greeted me warmly and drawing me in, invited me to sit. She fetched a second cup and saucer from her cupboard, moving around the small crowded room as if her eyesight was perfect. We chatted about school, about the weather and her health for several minutes. And then, in the pause that followed, I plunged in. 'Did you believe my grandfather was Jesus?'

She looked shocked. 'Oh, my dear, it wasn't like that at all.'

'What was it like then?' I asked.

'It was . . . it was . . . wonderful,' she stuttered, before feeling for the embroidered handkerchief she always kept in her pocket. 'But it was all too long ago.'

* * *

It was tough returning to school after the holidays.

'Did your grandfather really say he was Jesus?' asked one girl.

'It's none of your business,' I replied.

It was even worse attending school chapel the first evening, which, unlike Eden, was plain and the very essence of Presbyterianism. Two girls sneaked giggling glances in my direction whenever Jesus's name came up. My face reddened and my discomfort increased when Miss Burridge saw them and, in front of everyone, ordered them to her study after prayers, where they received a lecture and lost valuable house points for behaviour – at St Hilda's, one pupil sinned and the whole house suffered.

My fellow students had been asked not to talk to me about my grandfather but still whispered questions to me whenever they thought the teachers were out of earshot. 'Did he really?' one asked through a foam of toothpaste as we brushed our teeth in adjacent sinks. 'But he's dead, isn't he? So how could he be Jesus?' another whispered, under cover of flapping sheets as we changed our bed linen. 'Was he put in prison for blaspheming?' a third girl hissed, as desk lids slammed and chairs scraped across the classroom floor at the end of our weekly Latin lesson.

But soon they found more important things to talk about. Who would make the relay team? Would the strawberries ripen in time for sports day? Outwardly, I too threw myself into a constant round of athletics and debating societies – plus illicit activities, such as sleeping on the roof without permission and leaving the school grounds after dark. But inside I vowed to uncover the facts about my grandfather. Just what he did and, even more importantly, why. What I didn't realise then was how small a piece of the puzzle his astounding declaration represented; how many other reasons there were for my family to be thought 'peculiar'.

20

More Secrets Revealed

It was good to be home, with the long summer holidays of 1954 stretching endlessly before me – surely more than enough time to find my own answers. A plan came to me one night in bed. Perhaps I should look in an encyclopedia for facts about my grandfather. I knew when Ann had found out about our family's secret – like me, at school – she had had the intelligence to consult an encyclopedia there first. I sat bolt upright in bed in my darkened room – by this time, I had got over my fear of the dark and revelled in having a room of my own after spending term time in a dormitory with a dozen others. 'Why didn't I think of the school encyclopedias last term?' I muttered, as I switched on the bedside light.

Somewhere, a clock chimed three. I slipped out of bed, pulled my dressing gown around me, stuffed my feet into slippers and left my bedroom, closing the door quietly behind me. I crept past Mummy's room, paused briefly to listen for the muffled snoring contest between her and Gay, hardly daring to breathe myself for fear of alerting the Great Dane. I flitted down the front stairs, past the dining room with its door ajar, allowing moonlight to illuminate the long, tiled passage to the front hall. On I went, not worrying so much about noise now.

During long nights at school, racked with my new-found knowledge about my family, I had often lain awake as my friends slept. But out of those sleepless hours and those less-than-sterling school marks – it had been hard to concentrate last term – I had come to a decision. I would no longer beg others for information; instead, I would do what I did well: I would root, systematically and with the aim of finding as much written information as possible about my strange family.

The door leading to my grandfather's study was shut and the knob squeaked as it turned. I froze. But the only sounds were the tick of the clock on the mantelpiece and a hiccup from the room's radiators, as a trapped air bubble burped. Closing the door behind me, I crossed to the desk and switched on the green-shaded desk lamp. Too late, I noticed rectangles of light flood the lawn. I flung the switch, willing the light not to have been seen – even by a patrolling constable. Slowly, I dragged the room's heavy brocade curtains across the window and waited, apprehensive, before switching the light on again.

I started with the leather-bound set of *Encyclopaedia Britannica*. The tomes, their spines faded from a rich green to ochre, were displayed in an elegant *faux*-Regency bookshelf with long thin legs and its single shelf canted back so the volume titles were easy to read. It took no time to prise the first of the more-than-two-dozen volumes free and carry it to the desk. I turned the rice-paper-thin pages. With growing excitement, I came to the word Agape – and stopped, staring at the page before me. The next entry, which I was sure must be Agapemone, was missing. I bent closer and saw where scissors had sliced through the leaf of paper. I turned what was left of the page; Agar was the next entry. I was never to discover whether the cutting out of the entry had been an act of disillusionment, carried out in the traumatic period following my grandfather's death, or a more recent act of vandalism to prevent a young girl finding the answers she was searching for.

I was very tired during my first week home for the holidays. Even riding Pinto seemed an effort after I had been up half the night. But there was no other time in which to search my grandfather's study, where surely I would find what I was looking for – whatever it proved to be. But his desk drawers yielded surprisingly little: some old postcards, a hardly used diary with infrequent and mostly indecipherable notations. 'B from R, Xmas Day, 1913' was written on the flyleaf of a small, black volume for 1914. Underneath, in a different hand, were penned the words '*Homo sum; humani nil a me alienum puto.*' I am a man; I count nothing human alien from me. I whispered the translation as I flicked through the small book.

'Lovely day. Prayers in Eden 9 a.m.' was written for the entry on 1 January. 'Ruth a headache,' on 24 February.

In April, my grandfather journeyed to Norway, and in June and July, accompanied by 'Ruth' and chauffeured by 'John' – presumably my paternal grandfather – my grandfather spent a month touring the Continent. By the 17th, 'Ruth not at all well.' On the 28th, 'War declared by Austria against Serbia.'

The entries became increasingly difficult to decipher. Ruth was felled by increasingly frequent and painful headaches. The war gathered momentum – by September the 'Allies were advancing' and on 21 October, 'JVR went up to War Office.' But life in the Agapemone continued largely unchanged. The Christmas Day entry noted: 'Prayers in Eden. Dinner at five – sixty present' and 'Eden lighted fully by electricity for first time.'

In the memoranda section, under 'Books to read', my grandfather had noted *The Last Shot*, written by journalist Frederick Palmer and published by Chapman and Hall, and under 'To buy', *Our Good Slave Electricity* by Charles R. Gibson, plus *Rambles Round French Chateaux* by writer Frances M. Parkinson Gostling, published in 1911. Puzzled, I laid the tiny volume back where I had found it. The diary's entries seemed strangely prosaic for someone who believed he was the Second Coming. Where was the record of miracles and healings, or stirring sermons?

Under this diary lay another for 1919. As I picked it up, a page fell out. 'Very unhappy and dark times,' was written in my grandmother's handwriting in the tiny space provided for Friday, 15 August. 'It is better to die by one blow than to gasp out one's life by inches.'

The entry continued into the next date:

> Oh, help us, Lord; each hour of need
> Thy Heavenly succour give
> Help us in thought, and word and deed
> Oh help us when our spirits bleed
> With contrite anguish sore
> And when our hearts are cold and dead
> O help us Lord, the more.

Puzzled, I turned the page.

Sunday 17th: 'Capt. J.V. Read here for weekend.' John Victor Read – my paternal grandfather again. He seemed to turn up everywhere.

Monday 18th: 'Eight visitors left.'

Tuesday 19th: 'General society to one with a taste for seclusion is most irritating and wearing, nervous aversion to company.' Still true 35 years later, I thought.

Replacing the diaries where I had found them, I took myself off to bed as the numerous clocks began to chime four.

The next night, I searched through the piles of postcards carelessly tossed in a bottom drawer. This was more what I had expected: Exeter Cathedral, entitled 'Exeter Cathedral Across the Nave, Exeter Cathedral Choir and Exeter Cathedral, The Bishop's Chair'. There was a tinted one of the parish church St Mary and All Saints, Essex, with the title 'Rivenhall Church', and a glossy black-and-white postcard of the door of the west façade of Reims Cathedral with the caption 'The Great European War, 1914'. Underneath, there was a description of how this thirteenth-century door had been 'ruthlessly shelled and damaged' by the Germans in their attack on the city. Only one had been posted, and on it was a photograph of the Wye Bridge in Hereford, with the city's cathedral in the background. On the back was written: 'Very warm here, all going well.' It was my grandmother's handwriting. 'Tell John we hope to be back in time for him to go home in the C – so he can wait. Much love to all.'

Right at the bottom of the pile was the only other card with writing on the back. It was of a house shaded by a tree in a walled garden and taken from the street. Where the streets intersected, there stood a horse and cart. On the reverse were the words, 'With your precious one's love' in flowery copperplate. It didn't look like my grandmother's writing, but who else's could it be? And to whom was it addressed?

The next night, I abandoned the drawers for the Agapemone diary, which sat on the desktop. According to its printed instructions, this 'Year by Year' diary was intended to span five years, for the many 'who have neither the time nor the inclination to keep a full diary'. But even just a quick look showed it had been used since 1902. And I knew my mother and uncle still wrote in it.

It took almost a week to plough through all 336 pages, partly because some entries sidetracked me and I spent the day pursuing 'other lines of inquiry', as police dramas on television put it. I was little the wiser by the time I had finished, as the entries proved a confusing juxtaposition of world events and domestic details.

On 4 May 1912, someone had written: 'Ordered Claret Bordeaux – comes June 8.' On the same date, but in 1913, it was noted: 'Red flag of socialism in Trafalgar Square.' I turned to 5 May, the day of my mother's birth – and there it was: 'Life born 1.30 a.m.' So Margaret was right about the names! On 8 May 1904, I came across the entry: 'Sunday. Marriage BR.' Written beneath it, in my grandmother's writing, was: '1930, 26 years today since the marriage.'

Ten days later, on 18 May, the entry for 1936 read: 'Dear Katie passed away suddenly, age 84 years and 10 months.'

From the way people talked of this Katie, I had never imagined her to be as old – I calculated she would have been 104 if she had still been alive now. I decided to see if I could find a photo of her and so the following afternoon I searched through a faded green-suede-covered photograph album which lay among the sheet music in the dining-room piano stool.

I found one picture taken somewhere on the upper lawn. There was a group of about 25 men, women and children standing or sitting near what looked like linen-covered picnic tables. I was beginning to recognise faces easily after all my recent practice, even without the names, which, in this case, had been painstakingly written underneath. There was Toto, elegant in a wide-brimmed hat and Edwardian dress, seated at the end of one table, facing the camera and holding the reins of a donkey. On the donkey's back sat my uncle David, aged about ten and dressed in what was surely fancy dress: a cloak and hat under which he waved an enormous ostrich feather. Next to him stood Uncle Pat, who would then have been about eight, I calculated. He wore what looked like a white lacy dress and bonnet, and held a long whip and a stuffed toy in his arms.

On the other side of the group, I spotted my bearded great-grandfather, Charles Stokes Read, and near him a young Waa in a high-necked pleated blouse. I counted up the figures until I came to the one who must surely be Katie. She was standing next to my veiled grandmother. Katie's thick dark hair had been piled up above her heavy face, which looked older than most of the other women's in the picture. Almost as old as my great-grandfather, I speculated, even though her hair was not white like his. But her face was as lined, with those telltale rifts running from her nose to the corners of her mouth. In her arms she cradled a dark-haired girl of about five – my mother. She was leaning into Katie's shoulder, staring out at the camera almost as if she feared it.

But of all the entries in the diary, it was the one about my grandfather's death which puzzled me most. Not the entry itself; that was clear. On 20 March 1927, my grandmother had written, 'Our Dearly Loved and Very Precious Belovèd left us – in the flesh – after five weeks' suffering. Present R.D.P., Dr. M Frode, Douglas, Katie, Phoebe, Dora, Mabel, Waa, Millicent (12).'

It wasn't even the notation 'R.D.P.' I found puzzling – surely Ruth, David and Power – although I did wonder why my mother didn't seem to have been present. Was 16 thought too young? The names Douglas, Dora, Mabel and Millicent didn't mean much either. It was as I began leafing through the entries for the days following my grandfather's death that I realised something was missing. A good proportion of them stated how so-and-so had been 'laid to rest'. So why was there no mention of my grandfather being 'laid to rest'?

'It was such a terrible time,' Waa told me, when a few days later I asked her about my grandfather's death. 'We couldn't believe he was gone.' She told me again of the despair my mother had felt. How her sadness had led to clashes with her mother, whose grief had manifested itself in anger, especially toward her daughter. And how, at last, Toto had stepped in and offered to take my mother on a trip to her own relatives in the United States.

But it was years before I learned the details of my grandfather's bizarre funeral, conducted by one of the few remaining male members of the community, who wore a frock tailcoat and white bow tie for the occasion. And it would be even longer before I found what I considered proof that my grandfather had abandoned belief in his own Messianic claim – if, indeed, he ever had it – as demonstrated by the earthly will he left bequeathing all his worldly goods to his three children and their mother!

Bert Harris, who lived in the village and worked for the local undertaker, had been directed to make my grandfather's coffin. He told us how Belovèd had been laid to rest in an elm shell lined with white buttoned satin, padded with swan down and decorated with a mauve silk trimming. The shell was then lowered into another shell, this time lead-lined, and the whole thing fitted into a panelled-oak coffin with oxidised-silver fittings. The grave was lined with red camellias.

'It was a beautiful job, although I say it myself,' he told Ann and me during a tape-recorded conversation in the 1980s. 'It was the sort of thing that was done for kings and queens. I often wished I could have a photo of the coffin. If I'd had a mind, I could have made £100 from one of those reporters!'

He told us how he and the undertaker had outwitted the crush of journalists that had gathered outside the Agapemone the moment word of Belovèd's death had leaked out. 'We took the coffin out of the back door of the workshop, up through the garden, across the lane, through the wall and into the Agapemone. Then, when we had taken it in and everything was dealt with . . . we got old Joe Court to open the gates and we walked out with the webs, the trestles the coffin had been standing on – with all the accoutrements for a funeral.

'I bet they thought, "How did they get that thing in there without us seeing them?"' he chuckled. 'They wouldn't have known about the door.'

Bert told us how our grandfather had been laid to rest facing west – facing his congregation, who, like most people, were buried facing east. But, most of all, Bert endorsed what Waa had told me all those years previously: that the entire community had been devastated by their leader's death.

'It was the fact that he had died . . . a lot of them believed in it and then for it to suddenly have been all dashed. They must have felt dreadful.'

So confused, in fact, the grave had been left open for a full 24 hours after the funeral service. 'Which wasn't quite normal!'

* * *

I was beginning to lose enthusiasm for my search. I didn't even know what I was looking for, except that it had to be what I wasn't being told. I hadn't ridden my pony in at least a week and it was showing in his thickening girth and recalcitrance.

One morning, I was summoned out of bed by my mother and told to get over to the Ledermans as soon as possible. Pinto, no doubt bored by his lack of exercise, had done a bit of exploring on his own and had got himself stuck in our tenants' bathroom. He had wandered into the small ground-floor room early one morning, after the door to the outside had been left open. But once in, he found he couldn't get enough purchase on the slippery tiles to back out. It took Edward and me the best part of an hour to coax him from the house. It took me another hour to clean up the mess he had left behind. The incident taught me to temper my curiosity and I spent the next few days riding him through the surrounding lanes. But eventually there came a rainy day and I decided to explore Jericho once again. It had suddenly occurred to me the little Davenport desk, which stood on its own in the tiny attic room, could well yield some information.

And how right I was. Initially, however, I was disappointed when I raised the lid of the little desk. It seemed merely filled with a jumble of old sketchbooks, railway timetables and blank sepia postcards of obscure cathedrals. But as I rummaged, I spied a bundle of blue envelopes with telltale red-and-dark-blue airmail borders. The date stamp of the top letter was smudged, so I pulled out the sheets of flimsy blue paper and began to read:

> My darling Lavita,
> How I long to hold you in my arms again and . . .

I scanned the endearments, which sprang from the page, and began to redden. I glanced at the signature at the bottom of the letter: 'Your ever loving Polo.' I had stumbled on my father's love letters to my mother. Even though I hadn't seen him since I was four, I knew his writing well from the birthday card and cheque he always sent me.

Ashamed, yet strangely stirred by the letters, I read on. I had been taught never ever to read someone else's letters, but I had never seen anything like these; not even, I noted, the 'dirty bits' in the Bible, which my school friends and I read out to each other after lights-out in the dormitory, or in *Lady Chatterley's Lover*, which a friend had secretly removed from her grandfather's bookshelf and smuggled into school the previous term. I wondered how anyone could write such letters and still get divorced. Eventually, I crept away, not daring to return for a couple of days.

It was a member of the Kitchen Parlour who unwittingly came to my rescue. The woman had woken the previous night to find it had rained so much that the bucket that stood permanently on the attic stairs catching water from the ever-increasing leaks had nearly overfilled. Would I empty and replace it? This time, I turned my attention to the four small drawers on each side of the desk – at least I thought there were drawers on each side, then a knob came off in my hand and I realised the drawers on one side were fake. The top drawer of those on the other side wouldn't open either, until it gave way under my determined pulling and shot out to reveal a set of bone knitting needles, balls of string, a pair of tiny elbow-length gloves of the softest yellowing leather and the ubiquitous bezique cards.

The second drawer proved to be full of legs from assorted dolls, a blue square box of very musty sugar lumps, which even I couldn't bear to try, and yet more *Voice of the Bride* hymn books. The bottom drawer also jammed when I tried it. I squinted through the gap and glimpsed a sheet of heavy paper, which I freed with one of the knitting needles. It was a thick legal-size sheet folded in four and wrinkled and torn where it had been trapped. I smoothed it out and read the immaculate copperplate writing at the top of the facing fold: '11th March, 1915. Statutory Declaration of Edward Trevor.'

The paper crackled as I unfolded it:

> I, Edward Trevor of Bridgwater in the County of Somerset, solicitor do solemnly and sincerely declare as follows:-
>
> 1. That I was present with Fanny Davis of Four Forks Bridgwater, aforesaid and saw Ruth Annie Smyth lately called

or known by the name of Ruth Annie Preece and residing at
Four Forks near Bridgwater aforesaid sign seal and as her act
and deed in due form of law deliver the deed herewith annexed
and marked with the letter 'A'.

'A' was another long, stiff sheet of paper with the words 'Deed Poll' in
flowing script at the top. I spread it on the floor and, holding it down
with my elbows, read of my grandmother's change of name in 1915. I
read it again. And again. And a third time.

I returned to the first sheet and continued reading:

2. That the name Ruth Annie Smyth set and subscribed to the
said deed or instrument as the name of the person executing
the same is of the proper handwriting of the said Ruth Annie
Smyth and that the names Edward Trevor and Fanny Davis set
or subscribed thereto as the persons attesting the due execution
thereof are of the respective proper handwriting of me the said
Edward Trevor and of the said Fanny Davis.

And I make this solemn declaration conscientiously
believing the same to be true and by virtue of the Statutory
Declaration Act 1835.

Beneath was the signature of Edward Trevor and a Mr Barrington,
commissioner for oaths.

I sat back on my heels. Uncle David had been born in 1905, Uncle
Pat in 1908 and my mother in 1910. So why didn't my grandmother
take her husband's name until 1915?

A shaft of sunlight illuminated the statutory declaration and deed
poll documents spread across the warped linoleum. It was a full five
minutes before it struck me. Could this mean my strict grandmother
– who ruled my home with a rod of iron and whose word was law –
had never been legally married to my grandfather? Ridiculous! I had
seen the entries about their marriage in the Agapemone diary. This

was too important to ask Waa about; too terrifying to face my grandmother with; and too important to ignore.

* * *

I waited until the tea ritual was out of the way – Granny had a bad cold, so had kept to her bed. Tea had instead been taken in the downstairs drawing room. 'Come in,' called my mother, in answer to my nervous knock.

She was sitting in an armchair by the unlit fire, a gin and tonic in her hand. Uncle David was pouring himself a whisky from the heavy cut-glass decanter on the sideboard. He turned towards me.

'Granny wasn't ever married to my grandfather, was she?' I blurted out.

My uncle set the decanter on the silver drinks tray with a thud. 'Who told you?'

'A girl at school,' I lied. 'Is it true?' Neither replied at once. They didn't have to, I knew by their expressions. But I had to hear it. 'Is it true?' I repeated.

'Yes, Kitty, it is,' said my mother.

'Why?'

'He was already married,' replied my mother.

'What do you mean, he was already married?' I asked. And then, thunderstruck, 'He was a bigamist?'

'No, Kitty, there was no legal marriage. He didn't commit bigamy,' replied Uncle David, turning away to splash soda into his glass. 'But he might as well have done,' he muttered beneath the hiss of the siphon.

'But,' I began. I pointed to where the maroon diary lay open on my grandfather's desk. 'It says he married in there.'

My uncle's eyes narrowed at my slip. He opened his mouth to speak. My mother hushed him. 'It was a marriage . . . in the eyes of everyone here,' she told me quietly. 'But it wasn't registered. That means it wasn't legal.'

The silence swelled like a balloon. My mother glanced across at my uncle in silent appeal while he dabbed at his forehead with the silk hanky he kept in his cuff.

'So that means you are . . .' I raised my discovery hesitantly.

'Bastards!' my uncle interrupted harshly. 'Yes. And if you think you're hard done by, Kitty, you should try growing up a bastard!'

It was then I remembered another diary entry dated 11 November 1930. It was in my grandmother's handwriting. 'David to Somerset House for his birth certificate for passport; a difficult time for him.'

'Is that why none of you ever went to school?' I asked.

My mother nodded. 'No school would have us.'

'Weren't you lonely?'

'Often,' my mother replied shortly.

For the first time since coming to live in my grandfather's Agapemone, I felt I was being told the plain unvarnished truth. Not half-truths, not white lies. Emboldened, I asked, 'Who was my grandfather's wife then?'

'Her name was Catherine – you've heard us talk of Katie,' said my uncle.

'We all loved her so very much. In fact, you are named after her,' added my mother.

I was named after my grandfather's wife? Who wasn't my grandmother. *Her* name was Ruth and I lived with her. It was this Katie, whom I had never met because she had died before I was born, who had been his wife!

My mother told me how Katie had also been present at the 'marriage ceremony'. How she had attended the christenings of her husband's children by his spiritual bride. And kept the Pigott part of her husband's name, allowing Ruth the other half.

'Didn't Katie mind . . . about Granny?'

'She never seemed to, Kitty,' my mother said carefully.

'Katie was the most wonderful woman,' added Uncle David.

'I asked her once if she had ever been married,' added Mummy. 'I was about seven, I think.'

'What did she say?'

'She smiled and said, "I was once, dear."'

What hidden depths of sad acceptance are contained in her reply? A careful lie, designed not to hurt or confuse the child of her husband's mistress? The selfless act of a truly, good woman? Or one who had come to terms with her reality? And who, despite whatever private demons she wrestled, eventually reaped some reward in the love and affection she inspired in others, including her husband's children. And even his spiritual bride – judging by the sad entry in my grandmother's handwriting in the Agapemone diary for 18 May 1936: 'Dear Katie passed away suddenly, age 84 and 10 months.'

This upright, moral woman remains an enigma. Was she so devout she took her promise to 'take thee, John Hugh Smyth-Pigott, to be my wedded husband, to have and to hold from this day forward, for better or for worse' literally? Or was she, like so many Victorian novels would have us believe, secretly relieved when he 'set her aside'? Or perhaps she truly believed in this charismatic man.

And why did such a charismatic young clergyman, who had women literally falling at his feet, choose her? She wasn't good-looking like him. But she did possess a grace and a charm which attracted people to her. Was it precisely those qualities that attracted him and led to love, which died when he realised she would never bear him the children he longed for? Certainly it was her choice to continue to make her home in the Agapemone after she had been usurped by my grandmother. Letters from her sister offering her a home were produced in evidence at my grandfather's ecclesiastical trial in 1908 after he was charged with immorality. His trial, held in Wells Cathedral, Somerset, resulted in his eventual defrocking.

It took a couple of weeks before my uncles and mother felt comfortable enough to allow me to take tea with my grandmother. Even then, they chaperoned me. But they needn't have worried. I was far too scared of making my fierce grandmother ill to raise the subject. Besides, I found myself mesmerised when in her company by my efforts to reconcile this strict old woman and her position as my grandfather's spiritual bride.

'You're very quiet, miss,' Granny had remarked sharply, as she drained her second cup.

Three pairs of eyes swivelled, like interrogation lights, toward me.

'I've got a bit of a headache, Granny.'

'Nonsense, girl. People of your age don't get headaches. Get out of the house. Go for a walk. Get some fresh air.'

'Yes, Granny,' I replied meekly.

21

The Spiritual Bride

It all began with Louisa Fox, a devout follower who had started the Agapemone diary in 1902; it would continue until 1969. Louisa had fallen victim to 'visions'. These she eagerly related to Belovèd, who listened patiently and sympathetically. But when she told him of the 'special message' she had received, that he was to take unto himself a spiritual bride, Belovèd claimed he was appalled. He had no intention of taking a spiritual bride, he said, and refused to listen to any more of Louisa's messages. Then other followers began claiming to have had similar revelations. No doubt some hoped it might be one of them who would be so honoured.

And certainly, despite Belovèd's protestations and claims of agony and suffering over the idea, it slowly began to take root. (Not everyone believed his denials. The leader of a Welsh contingent of Agapemonites was to claim later that Smyth-Pigott was well versed in the art of seduction, having confided to him at least two years earlier that he had committed adultery with three followers, including Dora Beddow's mother Rebecca.)

Since the death of Brother Prince, Belovèd had been kept busy shuttling between the Somerset Agapemone and his Ark of the Covenant, where he would preach in the church basement to avoid unwanted attention. Even 18 months after his declaration that he was the Son of Man, his presence in the capital was enough to bring the sceptics out in force. It was while he was paying one of these secretive visits that he was stricken with a painful attack of kidney stones. His worried followers decided the safest option was to engage a private nurse.

Thirty-five-year-old Annie Preece seemed the perfect candidate. Not only had she trained at the famed St Peter's Hospital for 'stone and other diseases of the urinary organs', but she was available. Her previous client, the wife of Chancellor Chadwyck-Healey of the Diocese of Bath and Wells, had recovered sufficiently to no longer need private care.

And Annie had a mind of her own. She must have been intrigued to take on such a controversial patient. Perhaps she had already heard him preach. Perhaps she was a clandestine convert; it would hardly have been tactful to proclaim allegiance to the notorious Agapemonites while nursing the wife of a pillar of the established Church.

But from the moment they met, the die was cast: the headstrong nurse and the errant priest fell in love. For her, part of the attraction of this man, 17 years her senior, must surely have been his waywardness, which was mirrored in her own nature and which had already raised her from humble beginnings through domestic service to independence as a professional.

And for him, who knows? Many patients fall in love with their nurses, but did this middle-aged man – he was 52 – also recognise that here was a woman that not only aroused him but who might be courageous enough to take the fearful step he was now contemplating, thanks to his followers. For he must have secretly acknowledged to himself, if not to his 'spiritual bride', that their marriage was unlikely to remain unconsummated – however he justified it to his followers.

And in that case, perhaps, just perhaps, he wondered, could she also give him the children he longed for?

Excitement had been building for weeks in my grandfather's Agapemone by the time he escorted his spiritual bride-to-be to Somerset. He had prepared his followers carefully. 'For nearly nineteen hundred years He was fathering in the fullness of the Gentiles and working towards the consummation of His purposes in sanctifying the Church,' he preached, as he would continue to justify his actions for the rest of his life.

'When the Bride, the Lamb's Wife was called, she said, "I will go with this man." So the chosen of God are called to forget their own people and their father's house; to forsake the first creation and the world and its good opinion and its prizes, and to go forth and to follow this man. Not only to forsake, but to forget.

'But to you,' he told his followers, 'each moment is bringing you nearer and nearer to the full enjoyment, the full possession of your inheritance of bliss which God has given to you. It has not been a light thing to be cast out by the world; to be a speckled bird among all the others; to have whispers and looks upon you . . . But what do you find? . . . You find indeed that His service is perfect freedom; it is not a bondage, it is not a service of compulsion.'

He spoke at last of the woman he was shortly to introduce as his spiritual bride. 'She comes up from the wilderness of the world, from the trammel and the stress and the strife and the noise of the world; she comes up from the world leaning on her Belovèd, utterly dependent, hopeless and helpless in herself, but absolutely at rest, without fear, without doubt, without any uncertainty, she comes up from the wilderness leaning on her Belovèd and every moment nearing home.'

By his 'marriage' to Sister Ruth, the name he had chosen for the former Nurse Annie Preece, he would sanctify the union between church and himself, the Son of Man. And that union would represent forgiveness to the world.

Why Ruth? Like the biblical Ruth, Nurse Preece was a stranger to the community she was to preside over for more than 50 years. Once she had joined, she can also surely have had little idea of the depth of ostracism she would encounter for the rest of her life from society beyond the community walls. There would be no going back.

The couple arrived on the Saturday evening before the service. The estate was already filled with faithful come from London, Wales and even the Continent to be witnesses to this momentous event. No one seems to have had doubts about this taking of a spiritual bride, even though their leader had a perfectly nice and popular wife. Katie seems to have raised no objections and perhaps, in their innocence, these educated but gullible men and women thought the union was indeed to be spiritual, despite living proof to the contrary in the shape of Eva Patterson, the now middle-aged offspring of Brother Prince and his spiritual bride. But no matter how bizarre it sounds today, most of them – my Granny May being an exception – must have believed that the taking of a spiritual bride was indeed the final overcoming of the flesh by the Holy Ghost.

If the middle- and upper-class members of the community were excited, the Kitchen Parlour were, to a woman, beside themselves. Granny May, then lowly scullery maid Maisie Link, remembered the evening well, how all the servants had been told to assemble in the Kitchen Parlour after supper. Charles Stokes Read's daughter Millicent, a devout believer, had been a member of the party that initially greeted Belovèd and his spiritual bride and had promised to satisfy the anxious KP's curiosity.

'What is she like?' asked young Maisie.

'Oh, she's quite nice,' replied Millicent, 'but she's not a lady.' (As Aunt Tup would point out to us again years later: 'And, of course, she wasn't, was she? Not a gentlewoman, she wasn't.') It was to be some years before any of the KP would learn quite how humble Sister Ruth's origins were.

The night before the ceremony, the bride and groom exchanged wedding gifts of 18-carat gold watches. My grandfather's was a Swiss Hunter with enamelled Roman numerals picked out in rich blue, and on the back, in seed pearls and rose-cut diamonds, was the letter H, for Hugh. My grandmother's was a half-Hunter in the same style but with the letter R on the back. It still keeps perfect time.

The actual ceremony took place at seven the following morning. It isn't hard to imagine the scene: the early morning sun shafting through Eden's leaded windows adding lustre to the already highly polished floor and carving shafts of light across the scarlet sofas; the barely concealed air of excitement of being at the centre of things as the faithful filed in, the hems of the ladies' dresses sweeping the floor and the gentlemen, to a man, dressed in Edwardian frock coats or, at the very least, dark suits; the polite nods of greeting to visitors from afar, their presence yet another affirmation of the faith – as if one was needed. And into the very last rows of seats crowded those members of the Kitchen Parlour who could be spared from their duties, scullery maid Maisie Link among them.

Like the distant murmuring of a stream came the soft notes of the newly installed Willis organ, played by 25-year-old Dora Beddow. All eyes would have followed my grandfather's wife as she made her way down the packed aisle to a coveted seat on one of the scarlet sofas. Or were those present too caught up in their belief as to have totally suspended their disbelief? Was her smile of greeting a little fixed? Did her hand grip a little too tightly the arm of whoever escorted her? Or was she sanguine and in no doubt about what was to happen – the usurping of her place at the leader's side. Did my grandfather escort his spiritual bride? Or, like brides everywhere, was she brought to him? Certainly, she was heavily veiled and dressed in white.

The service would have followed the Anglican marriage service, with a couple of important distinctions – the hymns would have come from the aptly named *Voice of the Bride*, any reference to God or Christ was changed to Belovèd, and my grandfather played the part of both priest and bridegroom.

And what of Katie, his long-suffering wife? She never told anyone what she thought of her husband's betrayal, if indeed that was how she viewed his scandalous action in Eden that bright May morning – just as she never confided in anybody what she thought of being suddenly relegated to the position of follower in his Abode of Love. She simply went about doing what she had always done: living a quiet life without complaint, being a peacemaker whenever problems arose within the community and visiting the poor of the surrounding countryside.

Her stately figure, basket filled with food and simple medicines on her arm, could be seen daily around the village lanes, as she knocked on the doors of the less fortunate. When she wasn't helping others – and at the same time cementing support in the village for the Abode of Love – she submersed herself in her painting.

'Katie was an absolute sweetheart,' recalled one of my father's younger brothers, who had known her well. His view was universally echoed by others. She had lost her husband of 18 years to a younger and prettier woman but was to gain respect that bordered on sainthood. Would she have considered it a fair bargain? No one will ever know.

Perhaps Ruth's decision to accept the position of spiritual bride points to her passion for this older man – he was then in his early 50s and she nearly 20 years younger. My grandmother had never been a shrinking violet, but she must have accepted the consequences of agreeing to become my grandfather's bride in this way should she ever leave the community. Just as she must have known before she embarked on that bizarre adventure that Belovèd was married; it is likely that Katie had originally engaged her to nurse her husband through his painful attack of kidney stones.

But once Ruth took up the position by the side of the leader of the Abode of Love, she lost no time in putting into practice her ideas on diet and health. Within weeks of her arrival, she decreed that the huge and frequent meals community members ate were far from healthy and must be cut back. At first there was near mutiny among the residents, who were used to three large meals a day plus numerous snacks. My grandmother simply waited for the rumpus to blow over. It was Belovèd, and perhaps even Katie, who soothed ruffled feathers.

22

☙

The Little Unbeliever

Ann married John Buckley.

Entry in the Agapemone diary for
Saturday, 1 October 1955

My sister looked lovely. And happy, as she gazed into the eyes of her brand-new husband. They had paused for the traditional photo outside the church as two Royal Horse Artillery buglers raised their gleaming instruments to their lips.

Another photograph. This time of Ann and John laughing down at us from their seats high in the open horse-drawn carriage that would take them to the reception.

A third. Of his parents, with our father and Margaret and me, dressed in our full-length, moss-green bridesmaids dresses – my hair primped unflatteringly. But no mother.

I hadn't been surprised when, during the planning, both Granny and Waa had said they didn't feel up to the trip to Surrey, where the wedding was to be held. 'We're not young any more,' Waa had said with a smile. But the omission of Mummy from the guest list had come as a shock. I was told that Daddy had said he would not attend if my mother did. Ann was given to understand that it would be better if she did not have both of her parents present, so in the stultifying correctness of the 1950s, she opted for her father to give her away.

I had been hurt and angry for my mother. As I waved goodbye to her from the train taking me to Surrey, I felt a wave of sadness, glimpsing the flash of white as she raised her handkerchief to her eyes when she thought I was safely out of sight. What I didn't appreciate at the time was that my mother had been resigned to not attending following the appearance of an article in the *Daily Telegraph* in June that year headlined 'Three children of "messiah" in will case'. Jessie Fysh's brother and sister had contested her will (in which my mother and her two brothers had been named as beneficiaries of £10,000) and asked a judge of the Chancery Division to decide whether the gift was indeed charitable.

According to the article, the judge had asked what the tenets of the Agapemone were. That Smyth-Pigott had claimed to be Christ, they were told. 'Need you be told more?' the lawyer representing the old lady's relatives had replied. The judge was apparently waiting for the Smyth-Pigott's family to enlighten him as to the religious purposes of the church.

I didn't know my father and had convinced myself I wouldn't like him after he abandoned my mother, but when I met him in the days leading up to the wedding I instinctively warmed to this tall, good-looking and obviously military man. The way his huge dark-brown eyes twinkled when he laughed; the way he rubbed his fingers across his clipped moustache when deep in thought; and the way he leaned toward the speaker when he was listening. He would have been a nice father, I decided.

The realisation of what I had missed drove me to corner him at every opportunity. I was determined to get a few things straight and began to bombard him with questions, often rudely ignoring his second wife until she walked away. How could you just stop loving someone, I asked. Why had he married my mother only to leave her?

How disappointed had he really been in the prisoner-of-war camp when he had received word I was a girl and not the boy he longed for? Would he have stayed if the fourth baby had lived, the boy who had been miscarried after Mummy's fall just after my father's return? Why hadn't he ever come to see me?

He was both patient and honest. It was true he had always wanted a son, he said. But my being a girl didn't mean he didn't love me any less. And, no, he doubted whether he would have stayed had their fourth child lived. War and being a prisoner of war changes people, he said. 'Sometimes it's just too late.'

'But you never came to see me,' I said.

'I felt it was less confusing for you. And you have got to know Granny May.'

'But you stopped Mummy coming to the wedding.'

His eyes clouded. 'No, Kitty, it wasn't quite like that. I just didn't want a scene, for your sister's sake.'

I protested our mother would never make a scene, at the same time wondering just how she would have handled the wedding. 'There was no problem when Ann brought John down to the Agapemone to meet us,' I pointed out.

And there hadn't been. The old ladies had taken the visit in their stride. I had half-expected a flurry of activity in anticipation of the arrival of such an important stranger in our home, but there had been no carpet beating or floor scrubbing, the kind of thing that went on when guests were expected in the novels I had read. The days' rhythm didn't change, except for the smile on the old ladies' faces as they, to a woman, greeted me with, 'Your sister's bringing her beau down – how very nice,' or some such Victorian pleasantry.

Then, suddenly, there were the two of them, stealing a kiss at the bottom of the main staircase, my sister draped round a tall young man like a scarf, with a glow the like of which I'd never seen before. So, this was love!

I had decided almost immediately that I approved of her Captain John Buckley of the Royal Horse Artillery. He was tall and handsome, and I sensed there were few skeletons in his family's closet. Certainly no Messiah or Holy Family. Even better, he appeared to take our strange home in his stride, to Ann's palpable relief. He took tea with our grandmother, chatted with Waa and the old ladies as if he had known them all his life, and joined Mummy and Uncle David in the pub for a drink. He didn't even appear to notice Mummy finding it difficult to shape her words on their return, as if her lips had suddenly become partially paralysed. For her part, Mummy was quietly ecstatic. He was all she could have wished for in a son-in-law and she regarded my sister's forthcoming marriage as a personal triumph. All those sacrifices and all the attending loneliness had been worth it. Her eldest daughter was about to shake off her background – for ever.

On the second day of their visit, John had found time to help me wire up a light, fuelled by torch batteries, in my new rabbit hutch. I had wanted to do this for months but hadn't a clue how to go about it. The village undertaker/carpenter, who had been hired to make the splendid hutch as a birthday present, hadn't thought to add such a refinement. It took John less than half an hour to put everything in place. To finish the job, he said, all he needed was a light switch.

'I know where I can get one,' I said, and before he had time to question me further, I'd darted off, reappearing within minutes with a round Bakelite light switch.

He was about to ask me where I had got it when Ann interrupted him. 'Don't worry. Kit knows where to find anything in this place.' (I had unscrewed a live switch from the wall of an unused bedroom without giving myself a shock. Weeks later, when my mother happened to enter the room in the dark and was fumbling for the light switch, the jolt from the exposed wires sent her flying.)

Before I had left home for the wedding, I slipped into my pocket a photo I had removed from one of the dozens of albums filled with sepia portraits of Belovèd and his Holy Family. It was of a line of seven young boys and girls, ranging in age from about four to eleven years. The children stood one in front of the other in descending order of height, with their heads turned towards the camera. Behind them loomed Eden's white entrance doors and written in ink at the top of the photograph was the date, 1916. On the back the names of the children were noted.

Handing the photograph to my father, I pointed to the smallest child, a frowning dark-haired boy dressed in a white smock and knee-length shorts. 'That's you.' I said. I then pointed to the third in line, a young girl with long black hair, with black stockings beneath her white dress. 'And that's Mummy.'

'Good heavens!' My father gazed at the small photograph. 'That takes me back.'

'So, you were living there, too?'

'Not then,' he replied. 'But we had done. It would have been just after we moved away. We had come back for a visit.'

'It must have been amazing having all those children around.'

He smiled as he remembered. 'Yes, it was, Kitty. We had some good times. We often visited as children. I got on especially well with your Uncle Pat. He was great fun – and naughty. I remember how one time he rode his bike—'

'Through the picnic?' I interrupted. He looked down at me and let out a loud laugh that turned heads. 'What about Mummy?'

'Yes, she was fun, too, but she and David didn't like picnics like Pat and I.'

'Why did you and she . . .' I had been about to say elope, but his new wife materialised at his elbow and soon led my father away, insisting he must meet so-and-so.

* * *

The next time I stayed with Granny May and Great Aunt Tup in Cornwall, I went by train. This time I was alone, travelling in the guard's van so he could keep an eye on me.

I missed my Grandpa John's sense of fun, his lightheartedness and kindliness in the rambling, wisteria-covered house. My grandmother was very kind and a wonderful cook, too, but there still lurked that largely unspoken criticism of my home and a tartness to her tongue.

It took me a few days to pluck up the courage to continue my investigation into my family's past. It was Aunt Tup who brought up the Agapemone as she and I laid the table for lunch in the sunny dining room overlooking the sloping drive down to the lane. 'Do you remember, Maisie, the day I kept on making dear John stand on his head?' she chuckled. Turning to me, she explained. 'That was long before they were married. Maisie had brought me to live with her at the A—'

I blinked. 'You lived there as well?' Was there no end to the people who had lived in my home?

'Why, yes, dear,' Aunt Tup told me kindly. 'In fact, I wanted to live there for ever, but no one would listen to me.'

'And a good thing too,' Granny May called from the kitchen.

Aunt Tup ignored her sister's comment. 'I was only about six – it must have been . . .' She raised her voice. 'When would it have been, Maisie?'

'Before John and I married.' She appeared in the doorway, carrying a steaming rabbit pie. As she set it down on the table, her face softened. 'That day, when you kept making him stand on his head, and he said he would only do it if I wanted him to, was when I realised he loved me.' She dabbed the corner of her eyes with the hem of her apron.

As we lunched and during the rest of my stay, I brought the two women back again and again to their time in the Agapemone. I learned how my grandmother had had to be up at five every morning, stoking the old coal-fed ranges, and then spent every day until ten o'clock at night washing pots and pans in the huge stone sink in the scullery. How, in her rare spare moments, she, along with the rest of the community, had to attend Eden, where they were obliged to listen to Belovèd's rambling sermons. And how it was during one of those endless services that she and the handsome young son of Charles and Sarah Read had begun to exchange long, lingering glances.

Over the next couple of years, young John had pursued her with a determination that worried and confused her at the same time as it delighted her. She was sure consorting with one of the 'gentlemen' in the community – however outwardly egalitarian it was – would be grounds for dismissal. But her suitor insisted he was far from a 'gentleman'. Didn't he earn his living as the community's chauffeur and general handyman? Even his mother supported his suit. She had soon realised her son had fallen in love with the pretty little scullery maid known as May.

'When Maisie told old Mrs Read how she didn't think she was good enough for John, how she wasn't educated, Mrs Read said, "My dear child, you've got more education than any of my daughters – you can cook and keep house, which is more than they can do,"' recalled Aunt Tup.

And when May said it could mean a lot of trouble if she married John, Mrs Read had replied, 'There won't be any trouble when I'm alive. By the time I'm dead, you'll be able to cope with anything that comes along.'

'She had Bright's disease,' chipped in Granny May. This was a chronic ailment of the kidneys.

Aunt Tup took up the tale again. 'John used to go into the kitchen and help Maisie scrub the table legs. The cook used to say to Maisie, "You shouldn't let him do it." "Why not," says Maisie, "it won't hurt him."' She turned to her sister. 'That's just like you, Maisie!'

They told me about my grandmother's 'marriage' to my grandfather.

'We didn't know anything about her, except she was a nurse and had nursed your grandfather when he was taken ill with kidney stones in London,' Granny May said. 'The community received word Belovèd was bringing a very special person back to the community, who would be his spiritual bride.'

'It was all very exciting,' added Aunt Tup.

'Didn't Katie mind?' I asked, wondering at the weirdness of watching your husband marry another woman when you are still married to him.

'She didn't seem to. She had moved to the other end of the house a few months before, I think,' said Aunt Tup.

'But why did my grandfather "marry" my grandmother?' I was confused.

My grandmother and great aunt stared at me. They pursed their lips, exchanged glances and changed the subject, leaving me with the impression that, whatever the real reason, it had precious little to do with the 'spirit'.

'Look at the way he refused John and you permission to marry,' said Aunt Tup.

'Why would he do that?' I asked, growing more confused by the minute.

'Belovèd and Ruth had made the rule none of the young people should marry,' said Aunt Tup.

Despite my grandfather's bogus marriage to his spiritual bride, I learned the vast majority obeyed his ban on marriage – and sexual relations – including Grandpa John's older sister, Gladys, who was never to marry the love of her life, another member of the community. A scullery maid had been dismissed after marrying.

Not so my paternal grandparents who, with Charles and Sarah's support, managed to change Belovèd's mind and convince him he should marry them. This he did one Sunday evening in Eden. The next day, the young couple prudently went to Bridgwater registry office and had a civil ceremony.

'It caused a great deal of trouble,' recalled Aunt Tup. 'When they returned, Maisie was almost afraid to go to meals, the atmosphere was so unpleasant. She was sent to Coventry by the other members of the Kitchen Parlour.'

'Why?' I asked again.

Granny May explained the other young women, who all believed in Belovèd – 'Or said they did' – were angry and perhaps jealous that May had managed to persuade Belovèd to go against his own teachings. It was Belovèd himself who had eventually put an end to her devastating isolation when he learned what was going on. 'He was always very kind to me,' she admitted.

'What was he like?' I asked.

'He was tall and a good-looking man,' she replied. 'And he was very nice to me, even after I married.'

She told me how she had never for one moment believed he was the Second Coming.

'Maisie questioned things. Always has,' interrupted Aunt Tup. She turned to her sister. 'Do you remember you telling me how when you first went there to work, the old people told you to always put everything away in case you were caught up to heaven suddenly.'

'And I thought of all these old ladies with their full skirts and lace caps and leg-o'-mutton sleeves, all thinking they were going to float up to heaven,' laughed Granny May. Yet, she continued, Belovèd never held anything against her for her opinions, instead appearing to get a quiet enjoyment from the way she stood up to him. She recalled how one day she had been walking along the terrace path when he had come from the other direction. As he passed, he had laid a hand on her head, smiled down at her and murmured, 'My little unbeliever.'

'From that moment, that's what he always called me,' she said.

My paternal grandparents left the Agapemone in 1915, together with my Aunt Tup and the first of their two sons. Belovèd had wanted John to apply to be excused from service in the First World War on religious grounds, 'but your Grandpa would have none of it,' she said. Instead he joined the Royal Flying Corps and trained to be a pilot.

As I listened to these two women talk about their days in my childhood home, I marvelled at the strangeness of it all – and wished those I lived with could be so open. Particularly as, despite her memories, it was plain to me Granny May still harboured resentment at the way she felt Belovèd had taken advantage of her husband's family. She had grown to love her father-in-law and particularly his wife Sarah, who had taken her under her wing, helping to educate her in the ways of the gentry. She acknowledged it wasn't Belovèd's fault when her father-in-law was tarred and feathered, but surely, she argued, Ruth and her children should have handed over all the Read belongings, including the silverware, after Belovèd's death.

I left her comfortable home realising it wasn't just the war that had been a stumbling block to my parents' marriage: while she felt sorry for Belovèd's children and the unenviable life they led as members of the Holy Family, the last thing Granny May had wanted was for the favourite of her five sons to marry Belovèd's daughter.

But I also carried with me memories of my great aunt's high regard for those she had grown to love during her childhood in the Agapemone. 'They were lovely people. They were very unworldly,' said Aunt Tup. 'I think for a lot of them it was a wonderful refuge. They were safe there, they were protected.'

* * *

Returning home from boarding school, I found the estate shabbier and more unkempt than I remembered it. And when it came to money there was quiet desperation.

'So, that's that then,' sighed Uncle David. He and my mother were in the drawing room, having just finished breakfast He tossed the letter he had just opened towards her. 'There'll be no money from Jessie's will.'

'Somehow I never really thought there would be,' my mother replied quietly. But she sounded disappointed. The £10,000 would have eased their financial burden substantially. My mother explained that Jessie's relatives had contested the will and the judge ruled that the bequest was invalid.

'Can't you do something?' I asked.

'No, Kitty, we can't,' she replied wearily.

But Uncle David was ever resourceful. Somewhere he had met a man called Harold Nicholson. This Archbishop had become involved in spiritualism after the death of his infant son. He had joined the Catholic Apostolic Church, where he had risen swiftly through its ranks, before founding a religious organisation of his own called the Ancient Catholic Church. Why, suggested Uncle David, didn't they persuade Archbishop Nicholson to rent their father's Ark of the Covenant in London?

'But Daddy would have nothing to do with spiritualism,' my mother protested. 'And besides,' she added, with disillusion colouring her voice, 'even if we did rent it to this man, how would that benefit us?' The rent they would be able to charge – and that the Ancient Catholic Church could afford to pay – would no doubt only cover the church's upkeep.

'I'm sure we could find a way,' replied my uncle. 'And as Mama so often says, needs must when the devil drives.'

23

Births and Baptisms

Local farmer William Henry White, also registrar of births, deaths and marriages for the Bridgwater district, had never been inside the infamous Agapemone – and had no particular interest in doing so. He was a God-fearing man who stuck to the rules and was suspicious of those who didn't. But he was also fair, with children of his own, and so when Charles Stokes Read came to his office one morning in 1905 and asked him if he would register a birth in the Spaxton Abode of Love, Mr White felt it his duty to attend. 'He surprised me by saying it was a birth,' Mr White later told journalist F.A. McKenzie. The illustrated feature appeared in the edition of the *Weekly Dispatch* published on 27 August 1905.

On the appointed day, Mr White arrived at the Agapemone gates and was met by Mr Read, who ushered him into an imposing hall. He had barely removed his hat when a tall, thin man, with his black hair in a centre-parting and dark eyes, appeared before him, bowed and disappeared behind a red velvet curtain hung over one exit. That would be the Reverend John Hugh Smyth-Pigott, he said to himself.

'Come with me,' said Mr Read, who took the registrar to meet his wife.

'For a moment, I assumed she was the mother of the child,' White said. But only for a moment – Mrs Read was plainly past child-bearing age. 'I need to see the mother and the father,' he then announced.

'There will be only one name,' said Mrs Read.

'Ah!' He knew that code. 'Then she is single, and the child illegitimate.'

Mrs Read replied merely that he would be ushered into her presence directly.

Silence fell. Mr Read excused himself and left the pleasant sitting room. His wife indicated the registrar take a seat. 'You know, Mr White, this building was built 60 years ago by Brother Prince,' she began. 'He came to prepare the way of our Lord.'

Mr White didn't wish to get into a discussion on this strange place, he later explained to the reporter, but there seemed no stopping the lady.

'I prayed that I might see the Lord. That He might lay his hands on my head and bless me. That day has come. He is amongst us. This is one of the most memorable days of your life,' she urged the registrar. 'You will be ushered into the very presence of our Lord. You will see his face and touch his flesh.'

The registrar had heard the rumours. So it was true. These gentle, polite men and women actually believed the tall, thin man he had met a few minutes ago in the mansion's entrance was 'Our Lord'. 'I was surprised beyond words,' he exclaimed.

Just then, Mr Read returned and asked the registrar to follow him. Escorted by the elderly couple, White found himself guided along a narrow dark passage with many confusing turns until the little party stepped into a light, airy vestibule. Through a pair of arched glass doors came an excited murmuring. Before he had time to gather his wits, Mr White found himself ushered into a high-ceilinged chapel, the polished oak floor divided into two roughly equal sections by three descending shallow steps. Most of the seats, some scarlet sofas, others hardback chairs, were already filled with people. Above them hung a series of oil paintings of Highland cattle. What a rum place, he thought to himself, before realising he was surrounded by women: some of a certain age, others young and decidedly beautiful, he noted. At the far end of the chapel, a young woman reclined on a chaise longue studded with velvet cushions. The Reverend Smyth-Pigott, whom Mrs Read had referred to as 'our Lord', stood protectively to one side of the reclining lady. 'She looked quite beautiful,' he recalled later.

Seated beside the chaise was a nurse cradling a baby in white swaddling clothes. Mr White walked down the aisle between the assembled worshippers and approached the baby. 'I immediately noticed that it had a pronounced resemblance to the father, Smyth-Pigott.' There was nothing for it but to begin the process. The registrar turned to the Reverend and explained the procedure: how he must record the date of birth, parentage and baby's name. He opened the register book he had brought with him and placed it on the stand thoughtfully placed at his elbow. He noted the baby's date of birth: Friday, 23 June 1905.

'What is the baby's name?' he asked.

'Glory,' replied the father.

Mr White felt confused. He was sure he had read in the newspapers that the child was a boy. Oh, well, he had obviously been mistaken. Glory was surely a girl's name. 'Glory,' he noted and added 'girl' in the column signifying the baby's sex.

Smyth-Pigott, who had been watching carefully, reached out a hand and took the book and pen from the startled registrar. 'Son' he amended in his spiky hand.

'My son, Glory. Glory, my son,' he proclaimed in a loud voice, his eyes uplifted toward the ceiling.

'Glory! Glory!' chorused the rows of followers.

'Hmm!' Mr White cleared his throat; now for the next minefield. 'What is the name of the mother and how should it be written down?' He wasn't going to make the same mistake twice.

'Her name is Ruth Annie Preece.'

'Profession?'

'Lady. Just lady,' said Smyth-Pigott.

Mr White didn't like to think of himself as a prude, but 'lady'? 'I'm afraid that's not sufficient,' he countered. 'What is her profession now?'

'She was a hospital nurse.'

'But not now?'

The Reverend Smyth-Pigott shot him a glance. The registrar waited. They had asked him to come here, now it must be done right. 'Perhaps she is of independent means,' he suggested kindly. After all, he wasn't there to judge these people, merely to carry out his duty.

The Reverend nodded. Then, much to Mr White's relief, the leader of this strange community readily named himself as the father, even signing to that effect. Mr White was anxious to get the whole thing over and return to his office where ordinary people, from the highest to the lowest, came to register the momentous events of their lives. But the community hadn't done with him yet.

The Reverend gave a blessing and then Mrs Read came forward and addressed the registrar. 'You may now kiss the Divinity,' she told him.

Mr White blinked. The Divinity? Of course, the child! Well, why not? No harm in it! He glanced around, taking in the well-dressed congregation, and resisted shaking his head in wonderment. It was all so normal looking, and yet . . . He crossed the floor to where the nurse sat with the baby in her arms. She rose as Mr White leant forward and touched the infant's downy cheek with his lips. 'I complied with the request,' he later told the reporter – and much later the ecclesiastical court.

By the time Glory's younger brother, Power, was born, on the evening of 20 August 1908, Mr White had retired. Just under a month after the birth, Mr White's replacement, a Mr Sidney Wilkins Hook, was summoned and later recounted his experience to Frank Farncombe of *John Bull* magazine.

Mr Hook was shown into a pleasant sitting room by a servant. Minutes later the 'Messiah' appeared, accompanied by Charles Read, Douglas Hamilton and two females, one of whom was the lawful wife of the 'Messiah', Catherine, now portly and middle-aged. She stayed in the background. On his arm was Sister Ruth, the notorious spiritual bride and mother of the child.

'It is difficult to say which of [the two ladies] should feel the most ashamed of herself,' the journalist editorialised. 'Yet [Catherine Pigott] was able to complacently look on and see the registration of the child of a younger and more favoured rival without evincing any trace either of disgust or jealousy.'

Farncombe couldn't help noticing that even though Sister Ruth was nearing 40, 'she still retains some of the beauty which captured the licentious eye of Pigott, that expert in female charms'.

As with Glory, the baby's name of Power caused the registrar to pause and look up from his book. 'Yes,' Smyth-Pigott went on, 'Power and Glory shall be for ever within these walls.'

'Amen!' murmured Sister Ruth.

There was an immediate outcry once word of the second birth and registration had leaked beyond the community walls. 'Measures of a most drastic nature will be taken,' pledged the Bishop of Bath and Wells, in the *Weekly Dispatch* of 4 October 1908.

The bishop can have had no idea his threat would be taken literally by Londoner Michael Sale, who, within a month, had tarred and feathered the luckless Charles Read when he couldn't immediately find my grandfather.

In an opinion piece in the newspaper, Alfred Fellowes, Barrister-at-Law, described my grandfather as living the life of an 'easy-tempered Sultan' and outlined the options facing society in its desire to put an end to Smyth-Pigott's 'life of sensuality and luxury' in his Somerset Abode of Love. Entitled 'How Smyth-Pigott can be Prosecuted', Fellowes' article outlined three 'methods of attack', arguing that however outrageous Smyth-Pigott's claim to divinity, it was not a matter for criminal law.

'The best method of treating religious impostors is to give their dupes time to find them out. The dupes themselves cannot be prosecuted for incredulity, for if this was made a crime the prisons might have to be filled with voters after every election,' he wrote.

Neither, went the advice, was it wise to punish moral turpitude, save where the very young were the victims, which was not the case. 'To protect grown women from the consequences of blind infatuation is rightly considered outside the province of the law.' But, argued the barrister, Smyth-Pigott could be charged with blasphemy, although even that could prove difficult as blasphemy was a denial of the scriptures and, he pointed out, 'Smyth-Pigott does not deny them.' Perhaps he could also be charged under the Vagrancy Act, 'for using any subtle craft, means or device, by palmistry or otherwise, to deceive and impose'. The third course of action, argued Fellowes, was to amend the criminal law as it pertained to disorderly houses, but 'it must be confessed that the technical difficulties of shutting up the "Abode of Love" on this score are probably insuperable'.

In summary, Fellowes advised the best course of action was probably to ignore Smyth-Pigott, his Abode of Love and his gullible followers. However, the bishop had other ideas.

24

A Defrocking

By 1908, Charles Stokes Read's 26-year-old son Harold, who was by then a composer, had already attempted to distance himself from his embarrassing parents by adding 'Jervis' to his surname. One day he would leave his wife and children for one of his former music students, but in late 1908 his main concern was his parents and their known association with the infamous Agapemone. So, one November evening, Harold took pen and paper in his Royal Societies Club in London and wrote to the bishop pleading his parents be kept out of the now seemingly inevitable court proceedings.

The Establishment wagons were already circling the Somerset community; dozens of Smyth-Pigott's former religious colleagues and acquaintances, even members of his wife's family, had been subpoenaed to appear before a Consistory Court in the ancient Chapter House of Wells Cathedral in Somerset. The trial, believed to be the first of its sort ever held there, was to be presided over by the Worshipful Chancellor Chadwyck-Healey, C.B., K.C. – whose wife had been nursed by Annie Preece just before she met my grandfather.

Court officers had tried their hardest to serve Smyth-Pigott with a subpoena, attempting to force their way into the Agapemone or waylay him in the surrounding lanes. On 3 December 1908, the Reverend Fairfax Nursey, vicar of St Margaret's, Spaxton, scrawled a hasty letter to the bishop's legal team. The elderly vicar had no love for the scandalous community just down the road from his own church and was eager to help in the prosecution of its leader.

'If you are still desirous of personal service of the complaint,' he began, 'Mr Bradfield suggests that he might probably obtain access to the grounds on Sunday, during the time they are in the chapel – as the policeman on duty knows him and would station himself near – and when Mr Pigott left the chapel he would come forward and might without difficulty serve the notice [to appear].'

It didn't work. My grandfather successfully evaded being served, but my great-grandfather, the faithful Charles Read, volunteered to appear and accepted a subpoena in the naive belief that he would be able to speak on behalf of the man for whom he had sacrificed his wealth and position in society.

And the bailiffs weren't the only ones to call on the Abode of Love. On the evening of Sunday, 3 January 1909, Michael Sale, the man responsible for tarring and feathering the luckless Charles, once again entered the grounds. The community's rattled residents hastily sent for the local constable, who escorted Sale away.

A Mr Perris, news editor of London's *Daily Chronicle*, offered the bishop 'any of the information which the *Daily Chronicle* has in its possession with regard to Pigott'. He went on to say, 'We have been collecting evidence for some time and we should be glad to place it at [your] disposal.' The editor insisted that the deal with the bishop was kept private to maintain the objectivity that the newspaper's readers expected – or at least the appearance of it.

Wells Cathedral is one of the most beautiful of England's magnificent cathedrals. Set at the foot of the rolling Mendip Hills, it was awarded its cathedral status in 1245. Its magnificent West Front boasts the world's most complete record of twelfth- and thirteenth-century statuary, more than 400 of them and all originally painted in vivid colours.

It was here in the cathedral's medieval Chapter House on the morning of Wednesday, 20 January 1909 that my grandfather was to be tried *in absentia* on three charges of immorality under the Clergyman Discipline Act of 1892 and contrary to the 109th Canon issued by the Province of Canterbury in 1603. The charges of immoral acts, immoral conduct and immoral habits were designed to cover the births of Glory in 1905 and Power in 1908, as well as general allegations of an immoral life. The bishop, perhaps wisely, made no reference in the charges to his troublesome priest's blasphemous assertion that he was Christ come again.

Charles Stokes Read was nearing 60 when he toiled up the magnificent flowing stone staircase to the Chapter House, followed by his son John. Above them openwork tracery soared, their footsteps echoing as they climbed to the imposing decorated Gothic room where their leader was to be tried. Charles would surely have been attired in top hat and frock coat, beard and moustache immaculately groomed, giving little hint, except in the tiredness in his eyes, of his recent ordeal.

The previous couple of weeks must have been some of the worst in his memory. He was still recovering from his tarring and feathering, while trying to hide his aches and pains from his increasingly concerned wife. Not even Belovèd's loving cup ceremony the previous Sunday evening in Eden lessened this loyal man's sense of foreboding. It was Police Superintendent Williams who had arrived unannounced and served Charles with his subpoena – a task Charles later assured his leader he was pleased to undertake. Worse still, today was cold, very cold; a cold that soon permeated the blankets that John tucked round his father. Yet Charles toiled upwards, at last taking his seat towards the rear of the rows of seats at one end of the astonishing polygonal room.

Above father and son, as they arranged themselves side-by-side, soared the 32-rib vaulted ceiling, seeming to grow from the central pillar. Light poured in through the huge stained-glass windows depicting scenes of the Resurrection, and beneath them stood the canons' stalls, each with their own nameplate.

The proceedings began. Charles was called to answer that he had received the subpoena. As he resumed his seat, the prosecuting lawyer informed 'his Worshipful Chancellor' that the court had received no answer to the complaints. He went on to outline the absent defendant's career and that of his predecessor, the notorious Brother Prince, who, he remarked, 'under the guise of a so-called religion lived a life of blasphemy and fraud and immorality'.

Barrister Beverley Vachell went on to say that Smyth-Pigott 'claims to be the Messiah, the sent of God . . . They further claim that sexual intercourse is the highest form of spiritual worship.' But, he assured the court, they were not here to deal with these 'terrible blasphemies'. Instead, he concentrated on Smyth-Pigott's life to the point where he succeeded Prince and took his spiritual bride 'whatever that might be' to the Somerset community, where she gave birth to two children fathered by Smyth-Pigott.

'The Bishop was desirous, if the charges were proven, that this man should be cast out of the Church of England,' he concluded. 'It was a lamentable thing that this beautiful hamlet of Spaxton should be turned into a wilderness of particularly repulsive vice.'

The trail of witnesses called to bear out the facts laid out in the lawyer's opening statement must have seemed endless to the watching Charles: Belovèd's former religious superiors, even a clerk bearing Smyth-Pigott's signature to his oath of allegiance and ordination; his brother-in-law and sister-in-law, who testified to his marriage to their sister – and the fact that Catherine still resided at the Agapemone; the registrars of the births of Glory and Power, who were witnesses to Smyth-Pigott's and his spiritual bride's signatures claiming they were the infants' parents; and lastly journalist Frank Farncombe, who told how he had managed to get into the community and had persuaded the gardener to point out Sister Ruth. He continued his evidence saying he had interviewed Smyth-Pigott, who had told him that not only were members of the community 'above sin' but had said 'my wife is no more my wife than any other person here. We are brothers and sisters in the spirit.'

Charles could sit still no longer. Before his son could restrain him, the old man had risen painfully to his feet. 'There is no one here to defend Mr Pigott,' he said. 'May I say a word?'

The chancellor looked down from his lofty throne and addressed Charles. He could not hear him as no answer had been received to the subpoena.

'I would like to say what I think of the last witness,' persevered Charles.

A court official called out for order in the court. He went over to Charles and commanded he be silent.

It was all over in minutes. The chancellor announced that the case had been proved beyond a shadow of a doubt. Smyth-Pigott was guilty on all counts and must pay all the court costs, pending the bishop's final decision.

Six weeks later, on Saturday, 6 March at 2.30 in the afternoon, my grandfather was formally defrocked by George Wyndham Kennion, Lord Bishop of Bath and Wells, in an imposing ceremony within the cathedral. My grandfather did not attend.

'The scene was a striking one,' one newspaper reported. At least three bishops attended in full Episcopal robes, and the diocesan chaplain, the chancellor in a full-bottomed wig, registrars and priests proceeded through the choir to the altar rails.

'To some it must appear a strange fact that no charge has been brought against the defendant for the blasphemous utterances with which he has been credited,' began the bishop from his chair near the Holy Table. 'Upon this I would observe that there is grave doubt whether under the Clergy Discipline Act, under which the last proceedings were taken, a prosecution for blasphemy could have been included. If it could have been included, it is not easy to see how any other punishment could have been imposed than it is my painful duty now to inflict.'

The bishop then pronounced my grandfather 'entirely removed, deposed and degraded from the said offices of priest and deacon respectively'. Calling on the assembled throng, the bishop then prayed, 'grant to our erring brother true repentance and amendment of life, and to us and His whole Church pardon and peace'.

The ceremony was not noted in the Agapemone diary.

The following afternoon, Charles's wife Sarah passed away.

25

The End of an Era

Dear Waa passed away at 4.20 p.m. The greatest loss
to us. R.I.P.

Entry in the Agapemone diary for
Thursday, 1 March 1956

I should have known something was up when I received a letter
from Mummy. It was the first time she had ever sent one to me.
Waa hadn't been feeling well for the past few days, she wrote.

Two days later, Miss Lilian Burridge, the headmistress, pulled me
aside just as I was entering the classroom where we did our homework
each evening. 'I have some bad news, I'm afraid, Kitty,' she began.

Had my pony escaped and been hurt in a car accident? Had my
school fees not been paid promptly – again?

'I've received a telephone call from your mother, dear. Your nanny,
Waa – wasn't that her name – passed away this afternoon.'

'Waa's dead?' Not Waa! Surely not Waa. Waa was indestructible.
The bedrock of our lives. Always sober and always there.

'Your mother said it was very peaceful.'

No more cosy chats in her tiny, always toasty-warm bedroom. No
more being tucked in so tightly that my bed felt like a cocoon. No

more gentle smiles. No more rattle of the ancient sewing machine as she made my summer uniform dresses. No more Waa.

It couldn't be true.

But it was, and this time I didn't care what others thought. My love for Waa was absolute. 'After all, she wasn't your mother,' commented one puzzled fellow pupil. If some didn't understand why I should be so upset at the death of a mere nanny, then that was up to them.

Once again, the Misses Burridge showed understanding and allowed me to go home for the weekend; indeed, I could stay longer if I needed to.

There, I found a community in mourning and my mother in shock. Waa had been a member of her household for her entire life but for the period Mummy had spent abroad with my father; it was this gentle gamekeeper's daughter who had cared for my sisters when my mother followed my father to Egypt in 1940. She had been there for my mother through my parents' separation and divorce, and shouldered the family burden as my mother battled depression and alcoholism. Would my mother have coped if there hadn't always been Waa to fall back on? I'm glad I never had to find out. You only get one crack at childhood and mine could have been a lot stranger but for Waa.

She was laid to rest five days after her death in the now untended Agapemone plot in the graveyard of the Spaxton church, which bears the name of her patron saint, St Margaret.

But death hadn't finished with us yet. A month after Waa's death, almost to the day, and just as the Easter holidays began, my grandmother passed away. The doctor had been several times and after each visit the pall over my home deepened. The news soon spread and reporters began to head for Spaxton, as their forebears had been doing for the last 100 years.

It was a rainy Wednesday afternoon when the end finally came. Uncle Pat was due any moment. Mummy and Uncle David had been at Granny's bedside since the early hours of the morning. I wandered around downstairs thinking about what would happen to us all now that the strong-willed woman who had ruled this community from her boudoir for nearly 30 years was gone. As a small child, I had, to her delight, told my mother that Granny was like the hinge of a door – if it ever gave way, the whole door would fall off.

I watched the local doctor climb the stairs to her bedroom for the last time, only to emerge minutes later with my mother and uncle. 'She's gone, Kitty,' said my mother, dabbing at her eyes. Uncle David wept openly beside her. I wept too, but without that overwhelming feeling of loss I had known at Waa's death. And I wasn't prepared for the furore that greeted my grandmother's death – none of the other old ladies' passings had attracted more than momentary attention from outsiders; it had become decidedly routine for me. My grandmother had left instructions for a Christian burial and said she wanted to be laid to rest beside my grandfather beneath the chapel floor.

But who would give the spiritual bride of a self-styled 'Messiah' a Christian burial? Certainly not the Anglican Church, which already felt it had been more than accommodating by allowing my grandfather's followers to be buried in the cemetery of the village church. Besides, Eden wasn't consecrated and the local bishop had no intention of sanctifying a bizarre place of worship used by a defrocked Anglican priest who had proclaimed he was Jesus Christ come again.

Being buried in ground that has not been consecrated wasn't – and still isn't – illegal in England, but my mother and uncles feared it would only increase the inevitable publicity. I wondered why, when so many 'faithful', including my great-grandfather and great-grandmother, had already been laid to rest in various parts of the garden.

The questions grew even more bizarre. Even if they were able to fulfil their mother's last wish, how should she be laid to rest? In the normal manner with her feet facing east, or should she be buried facing west, like my grandfather had been, in his capacity as the Second Coming? And the locals had long believed my grandfather had been buried standing up; that he had even been laid to rest without a lid on his extraordinarily ornate coffin. Frequenters of the Lamb Inn speculated over their pints of scrumpy whether he might not have vanished altogether, having risen again.

'Did you get down to the original coffin [containing Belovèd]?' villager Bert Harris asked the undertaker the day before the funeral.

'Yes,' was the reply, 'and I can assure you that the lid was still on, because I stood on it.'

My mother and uncles eventually decided Eden would have to be consecrated – and who better to do it than the founder of the obscure religious sect who had agreed to lease the London Ark of the Covenant. Late that night, David telephoned His Grace, the Most Reverend Doctor Harold Percival Nicholson, Archbishop of Karim, of the Ancient Catholic Church, and asked if he would not only consecrate Eden but also conduct my grandmother's funeral.

'Pinto needs exercise,' I announced the morning before the funeral, set for Tuesday, 10 April, six days after my grandmother's death. I had had enough of the whole thing and decided to go for a ride far away from the persistent ringing of the telephone – 'Reporters again,' my uncle would mutter – and the endless huddled conferences. Even the old ladies seemed fearful of what would happen to them now 'dear Ruth' had passed over.

'Don't go out, Kitty,' warned Uncle David.

'Why not?'

An irritated look flashed across his face. 'For once in your life, Kitty, just do as I say,' he shouted as he rushed to answer the telephone again.

But when I went to catch Pinto, he turned tail and galloped off to the other end of the upper lawn. I couldn't even get near him. I finally got the halter on and led my snorting, dancing pony back to the stableyard. 'What's the matter with you?' I delved into my pocket for my last carrot and rubbed his nose while he stared out of wild eyes.

Eventually he had calmed down enough for me to saddle up and we set off down the drive to the small side door. I slid the freshly oiled bolt back and threw open the door.

Flash bulbs blinded me. I was left with the impression of trilby hats, inquisitive eyes and notebooks.

'Who will be conducting—'

'Will she be buried standing up?'

A jerk on the reins I had looped over one arm pulled me back as Pinto, spooked by the flashes and the sudden raised voices, reared and began to scramble backwards, his metal shoes slipping on the granite doorstep as he pulled me with him. The door was slammed shut and the bolt shot by Edward, who had been hurrying behind me to warn me about what was waiting.

'Them damn reporters have already made a nuisance of themselves at the Ledermans. And I caught one of them halfway over the wall. I reckon that was what spooked the pony,' he said as he ran to Pinto's head. He grinned. 'The dog nearly pulled the backside out of his trousers.'

That evening the man who was to consecrate the chapel and conduct my grandmother's funeral arrived wearing an archbishop's mitre, and robes of red and gold. Behind him followed his chaplain, dressed in ankle-length robes of a lesser magnificence.

'We're having such a time with the reporters,' whispered my mother as she and David hurried to keep up with the archbishop. She sounded almost excited at this brief return to the drama and exclusiveness she had known when her father was alive.

The little procession wound its way down the narrow passage to the chapel, the distant strains of the organ in the background. Eden was aglow with electric light, hardly recognisable as the dusty, moth-eaten Eden I knew. The soft glow of candles gave lustre to the Lalique vase, as well as the now highly polished floor, and depth to the paintings of Highland cattle that adorned the walls. Against this backdrop even the faded scarlet velvet sofas looked fresh. I breathed in, inhaling furniture polish and – was that Easter lilies? At the far end of the chapel, to one side of the open vault and flanked by banks of flowers, stood my grandmother's coffin.

The service of consecration had been private, but the funeral the following day was open not only to the community but to those members of the village who had known my grandmother through her long life. Even one of the small crowd of newspaper reporters was given a ringside seat.

'The Archbishop led the congregation in the singing of the 23rd Psalm to the setting of Crimond,' reported the *Bridgwater Mercury* on Tuesday, 17 April 1956:

> This was followed by the lighting of the altar candles and the burning of incense. In his address, the Archbishop referred to the kindly and generous qualities of Mrs Smyth and he emphasised the value of love in dealing with people. 'Love those who hate you,' he said.
>
> During the committal, Holy water was sprinkled on the coffin, and the congregation sang, 'The Day Thou Gavest Lord is Ended' – the favourite hymn of Mrs Smyth.

As I watched from the seat I had chosen at the back of the chapel, I saw Violet Morris, tears streaming down her face, turn to Bert Harris.

'Oh, Mr Harris, how sad I am.'

'Are you? Why?'

'If only they had had Reverend Graham – if only he had taken this service, how much better it would have been.'

She, like the rest of my grandfather's elderly followers, disliked the 'popish' atmosphere of the service, preferring the simpler order of service of the Anglican Church that my grandfather, and his predecessor, had followed (where Belovèd, of course, was substituted in all references to God or the Holy Ghost).

But my grandparents weren't allowed to rest in peace together beneath Eden's floor for many years. The chapel would be sold in early 1971, one of the conditions of the sale being that their remains were removed. Desperate for another injection of funds, my mother and Uncle Pat had had their parents' coffins exhumed and moved, most likely to the Agapemone burial plot in St Margaret's churchyard in Spaxton. It would be 40 years before I unearthed this sad little fact.

In the days following the funeral, I was given my grandmother's gold half-Hunter pocket watch.

My grandmother's death, aged 87, marked the end of my childhood home. The following year, Toto, Emily Hine and Violet Morris died. They were soon followed by almost all of the old ladies I had known as a child. Olive Morris sold the East Gate and moved into the laundry, where she was looked after by the two surviving members of the Kitchen Parlour. Soon, my mother and a housekeeper were the only inhabitants of the main house, the housekeeper in the west wing and my mother in the east wing.

The formal end came on St Valentine's Day 1962, when Uncle David returned briefly to sign the deed of sale before leaving for his old Mediterranean haunts. Eden would later become a television studio for a time where children's programmes would be made, such as *Toytown*, but is now a private house. The estate would be broken up, sold off in parcels and renamed Barford Close.

I had returned home to help my mother move her belongings from the main house to the small two-bedroomed cottage that, for so many years, had been home to the Ledermans. They had moved on in 1959 with their growing family to a larger and more comfortable house on the outskirts of Bridgwater.

Every one of more than 20 bedrooms in the main house had already been cleared, leaving telltale patches where pictures had hung and squares of dust where the furniture had stood. Even the Persian runner on the landing had been rolled up and carried away, so that our footsteps echoed eerily as my mother and I moved from room to room, checking that everything was ready for the auction sale the following day – and saying our goodbyes.

That day, we made our way downstairs to where the furniture was piled high in every room and assembled in the corridors, leaving just enough room to squeeze past: Georgian tallboys, Victorian chairs, desks, beds and even the upright piano from the dining room. Baskets of silverware sat cheek by jowl with a vast array of pots, pans and a collection of huge Victorian moulds; mahogany-backed bristle shoe-cleaning brushes of every size and shape overflowed from a cardboard box dumped next to a collection of mousetraps, which I poked with interest, feeling a flicker of satisfaction that the old-fashioned steel lobster-cage-shaped trap, complete with the tiny skeleton of a rodent that I had found in the hayloft all those years ago, was not included. But I did find a satinwood dressing box filled with crystal silver-topped bottles that I had been given by Emily. Too late, it had already been numbered and catalogued.

As I watched the curious shuffle through my home during the public viewing that afternoon, poking and prying, I felt both violated and relieved. I shared my mother's sadness at this final public indignity, the disintegration of her home. And yet, to have this increasingly ramshackle estate gone for good, when it had hung like a millstone around my mother's neck, meant that surely we could all truly put it behind us.

While we sat before the electric fire in the cottage's tiny sitting room that last evening before the sale, my mother talked about how hard she had tried to escape the shackles of her Holy Family and never succeeded.

'It wasn't to be,' she said.

'But we have escaped,' I replied.

She smiled and drew herself up, permitting a brief moment of pride. 'Yes, I believe you have.'

That feeling of accomplishment, of having given her own children what she had never had – a life beyond the high stone walls of her father's Abode of Love – was what would sustain her in the face of tragedy. In 1964, two years after the sale of my childhood home, her beloved brother, David, was murdered in Tangier, where he lies in an unmarked, and possibly communal, grave.

'I hadn't the heart to tell her,' a friend of mine confessed during a visit to my mother. This friend had recently returned from Tangier and had spent a day searching for my uncle's grave.

My mother died in 1979, just months before I emigrated to Canada. Uncle Pat died in 1985.

Epilogue

It seemed fitting that it was twilight that early summer evening in 2005 when I last strolled through the grounds of my childhood home. I was joined by Pam, the school friend who, all those years before, had been caught with me sliding on cushions in Eden. The forbidding entrance gates are no more. We strolled in past the darkening silhouette of the mansion, now divided into three sizable houses. When we rounded the corner of the building, Pam stopped in surprise. What used to be acres of lawn leading up to the path, where we would ride our ponies, our bicycles and play catch, were no more. Instead there are bungalows set in neat postage-stamp gardens; even the stables have been converted into a house.

'Good heavens!' she exclaimed.

'I know. It's very different, isn't it?' I replied.

A young couple were gathering up plastic toys from their garden beneath the windows of the former dining room, the room where Emily had thrown the vegetable dish – and unwittingly started me on my quest.

It was good to see my childhood home restored into village life after more than a century and lay to rest the ghosts of those gullible souls who had turned their backs on the world to follow my charismatic grandfather and his dreams of . . . glory? salvation? an earthly paradise? Did he even continue to believe in his self-proclaimed divinity, or did he find himself trapped by those beliefs in his luxurious Abode of Love? For it would surely have been impossible for him to declare to the faithful, and especially his Holy Family, that he had got it wrong, that he wasn't the Son of Man after all.

I believe that was precisely his predicament in later years, surely proven by the presence of a will. Now, I realise it was disillusion that I sensed in those dark sad eyes and those deeply carved furrows that ran from his nose to the corners of his lips. And his legacy to me? It is a lifelong disinterest in religion and a suspicion of charismatic people, who so often prey on the gullible. Is that what my grandfather and his predecessor did? Yes, but perhaps in their defence it can be argued that in the beginning they each believed their own teachings.

As Pam and I retraced our steps, I noticed lights glowing through Eden's windows. I felt a frisson of uneasiness; I saw the former chapel as it must have appeared that night in 1908 when the intruders who tarred and feathered my paternal great-grandfather targeted it. They had waited outside watching the community file out of Eden, its yellow light emanating through the stained glass. The feeling went as quickly as it had come – Eden was no target now but a home. Thank God for that.

With one last glance, we set off for the camaraderie awaiting us at the Lamb Inn, where my husband and more former school friends were waiting for us. It was inevitable that the talk turned eventually to the Agapemone and what had happened to everyone who had lived there. Then someone asked me about my name. Why was I now known as Kate instead of Kitty, the name they all knew me by? Was it to distance myself from my strange childhood?

I told them I had started calling myself Kate after I had left home, simply because it sounded more grown-up. But afterwards I thought again about my answer – was that all there was to it? I think so!

But this isn't quite the end of my story. For Ann, Margaret and me, the last tangible link with our grandfather's Abode of Love still stands on Rookwood Road in north London, known as the Cathedral Church of the Good Shepherd by the small body of adherents of the Ancient Catholic Church. To our surprise, the Charity Commission for England and Wales recently contacted Ann to say that the purposes of the Agapemonites and thus their church was never exclusively charitable; that it had been wrongly registered. Our grandfather's Ark of the Covenant was therefore being removed from the register.

My sisters and I have learned that nothing is ever straightforward about our family history. Our grandfather's church in north London is no exception. The fact that the building is no longer a registered charity brings new challenges and fresh complications that we are only now starting to appreciate. It is far too early to speculate on the future of this extraordinary building, but perhaps, when all is said and done, we will find a way for the pipe organ, built by the famous Henry Willis and Sons Ltd, to be enjoyed by more than the small congregation that worships there each week. Just as it would be wonderful for those voluptuous Song of Solomon stained-glass windows to be more widely seen.

Who knows what the future will bring.

One thing remains constant, however, and that is the reaction we get whenever we attempt to explain our strange family and its even stranger church: the raised eyebrows, the unconscious blink of surprise. The expression carefully composed to not reveal astonishment or rude disbelief.

Then again, I suppose my sisters and I shouldn't be surprised. Skeletons in the family cupboard are one thing – Messiahs quite another.

MY FAMILY TREE

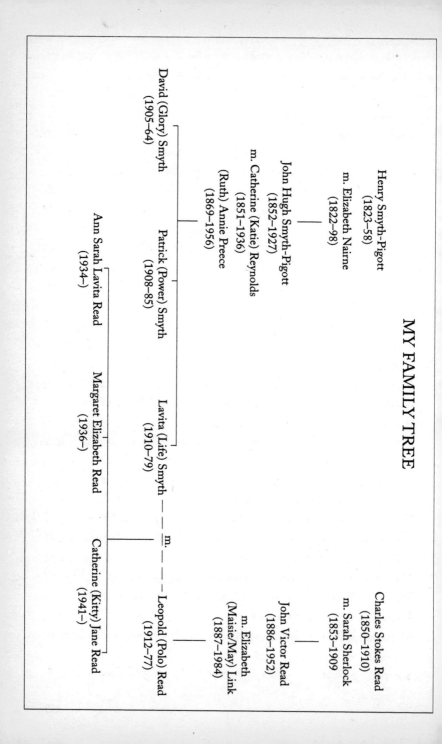

Henry Smyth-Pigott
(1823–58)

m. Elizabeth Nairne
(1822–98)

Charles Stokes Read
(1850–1910)

m. Sarah Sherlock
(1853–1909)

John Hugh Smyth-Pigott
(1852–1927)

m. Catherine (Katie) Reynolds
(1851–1936)

(Ruth) Annie Preece
(1869–1956)

David (Glory) Smyth
(1905–64)

Patrick (Power) Smyth
(1908–85)

Lavita (Life) Smyth
(1910–79) — — — m. — — — — Leopold (Polo) Read
(1912–77)

John Victor Read
(1886–1952)

m. Elizabeth
(Maisie/May) Link
(1887–1984)

Ann Sarah Lavita Read
(1934–)

Margaret Elizabeth Read
(1936–)

Catherine (Kitty) Jane Read
(1941–)

Select Bibliography

BOOKS

Baker-Carr, C.D.T. 'The Bogus Messiah' in *The World's Strangest Stories* (*London Evening News*, 1955)

Dixon, William Hepworth *Spiritual Wives* volumes 1 and 2 (originally published by Hurst and Blackett, London, 1868; reprinted in an unabridged facsimile by Elibron Classics of Adamant Media Corporation, vol. 1 [2000], vol. 2 [2001])

Knox, Ronald A. *Enthusiasm* (Oxford University Press, 1950)

Mander, Charles *The Reverend Prince and His Abode of Love* (EP Publishing, 1976)

Matthews, Ronald *English Messiahs* (Methuen & Co. Ltd, 1936)

McCormick, Donald *Temple of Love* (The Citadel Press, 1965)

Menen, Aubrey *The Abode of Love* (Scribners, 1956)

Montgomery, John *Abodes of Love* (Putnam and Company Ltd, 1962)

Schwieso, Joshua *Deluded Inmates, Frantic Ravers and Communists; A*

Sociological Study of the Agapemone, a Sect of Victorian Apocalptic Millenarians (unpublished Ph.D. thesis, 1994)

Smyth-Pigott, John Hugh *Extempore Addresses* (privately printed, 1936)

NEWSPAPERS AND MAGAZINES

Kingsland and Hackney Gazette

Morning Leader

Weekly Dispatch

John Bull

Somerset County Herald

Central Somerset Gazette

Ross Gazette

Bridgwater Mercury

Bridgwater Times

Daily Express

Daily Mail

British Weekly

Berkshire Chronicle

The Times

Western Daily Press

Evening Post

Somerset Magazine

Bristol Times

OTHER SOURCES

Beloved, episode from the Victorian Scandals series focusing on the Abode of Love (aired on 10 October 1976, Granada)